To Tommy
I hope y
book

# I Believe in Miracles

*Leslie Kessler* (signature)

Leslie Kessler

CROSSBOOKS
PUBLISHING

CrossBooks™
A Division of LifeWay
1663 Liberty Drive
Bloomington, IN 47403
www.crossbooks.com
Phone: 1-866-879-0502

First published by CrossBooks 10/3/2013

ISBN: 978-1-4627-3169-5 (sc)
ISBN: 978-1-4627-3168-8 (hc)
ISBN: 978-1-4627-3170-1 (e)

Library of Congress Control Number: 2013917148

Printed in the United States of America.

This book is printed on acid-free paper.

Scripture taken from the Holy Bible, New International Version®, NIV®. Copyright © 1973, 1978, 1984, 2011 by Biblica, Inc.™ Used by permission of Zondervan. All rights reserved worldwide. www.zondervan.com The "NIV" and "New International Version" are trademarks registered in the United States Patent and Trademark Office by Biblica, Inc.™

Scripture taken from the King James Version of the Bible.

# TABLE OF CONTENTS

# Leslie John Kessler Family Tree - 2013

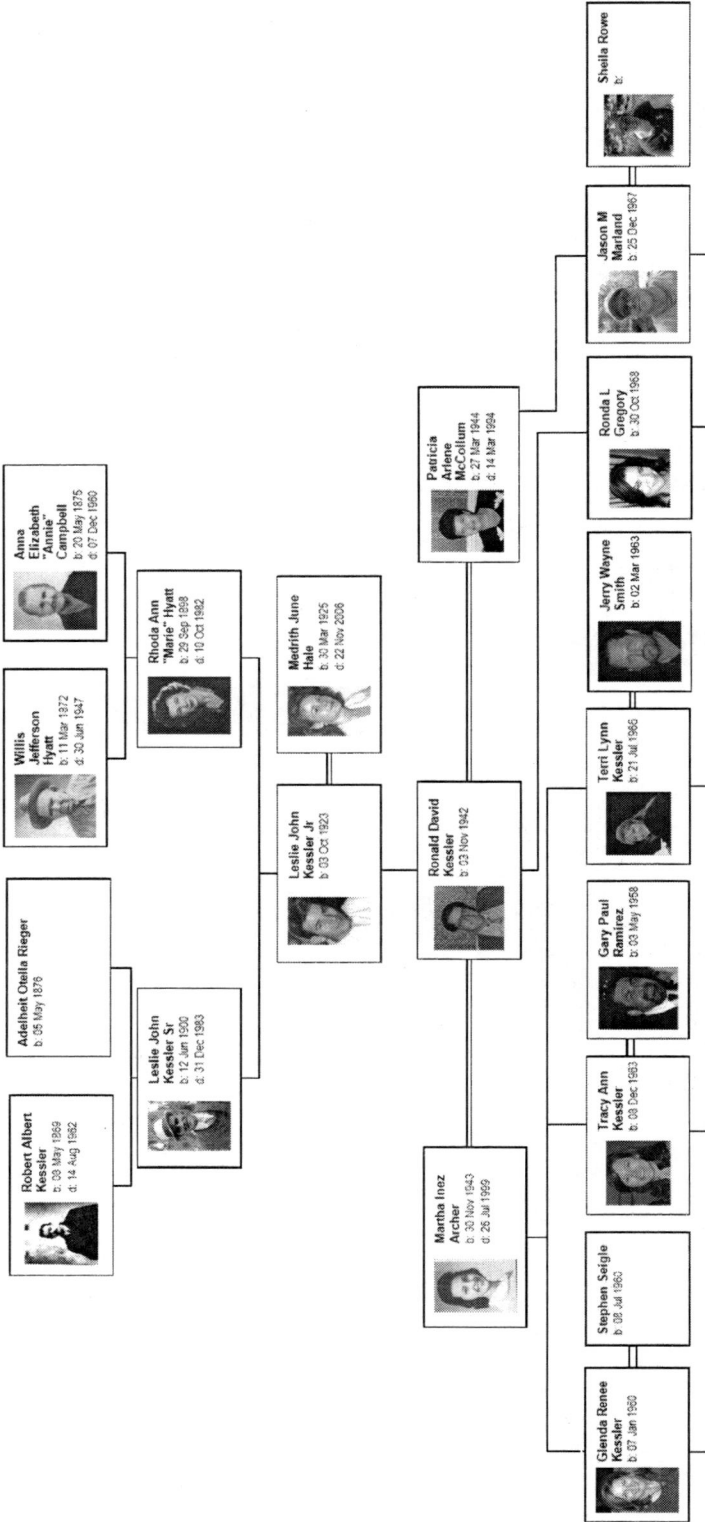

**Robert Albert Kessler**
b: 08 May 1869
d: 14 Aug 1962

**Adelheit Otella Rieger**
b: 05 May 1876

**Willis Jefferson Hyatt**
b: 11 Mar 1872
d: 30 Jun 1947

**Anna Elizabeth "Annie" Campbell**
b: 20 May 1875
d: 07 Dec 1960

**Leslie John Kessler Sr**
b: 12 Jun 1900
d: 31 Dec 1983

**Rhoda Ann "Marie" Hyatt**
b: 29 Sep 1898
d: 10 Oct 1982

**Leslie John Kessler Jr**
b: 03 Oct 1923

**Medrith June Hale**
b: 30 Mar 1925
d: 22 Nov 2006

**Martha Inez Archer**
b: 30 Nov 1943
d: 26 Jul 1969

**Ronald David Kessler**
b: 03 Nov 1942

**Patricia Arlene McCollum**
b: 27 Mar 1944
d: 14 Mar 1994

**Glenda Renee Kessler**
b: 07 Jan 1960

**Stephen Seigle**
b: 08 Jul 1960

**Tracy Ann Kessler**
b: 08 Dec 1963

**Gary Paul Ramirez**
b: 03 May 1958

**Terri Lynn Kessler**
b: 21 Jul 1966

**Jerry Wayne Smith**
b: 02 Mar 1963

**Ronda L Gregory**
b: 30 Oct 1968

**Jason M Marland**
b: 25 Dec 1967

**Sheila Rowe**
b:

## Jason M Marland/Shelia Rowe

**Mariah Leann Kennebrew**
b: 28 Sep 1992

**Joshua Aaron Marland**
b: 30 Jan 2001

**Jacob Patrick Marland**
b: 09 Sep 2009

## Ronda L Gregory

**Cassandra Kennedy**
b: 27 Dec 1988

**Jessica Kennedy**
b: 02 Mar 1991

**Megan Gregory**
b: 16 Sep 1994

**Matthew Gregory**
b: 14 May 1998

## Terri L Kessler/Jerry W Smith

**Jerry Wayne Smith Jr**
b: 04 Jan 1985

**Lacie Lanette Smith**
b: 17 Feb 1989

**Calie Lynn Smith**
b: 13 Jan 2010

## Tracy A Kessler/Gary P Ramirez

**Tiana Renee Ramirez**
b: 16 Nov 1980

**Brian J Darling**
b: Abt. 1977

**Rachel Ann Ramirez**
b: 21 Oct 1983

**Sydney June Ramirez**
b: 09 Apr 1994

**Kennedy Darling**
b: 25 Feb 2008

**Jameson Thomas Darling**
b: 11 Jun 2010

## Glenda R Kessler/Stephen Seigle

**Kevin Scott Seigle**
b: 19 Jul 1982

**Craig Anthony Seigle**
b: 20 Jun 1986

**Lauren Michelle Reeger**
b: 19 Oct 1985

**Leslie Marie Seigle**
b: 31 Mar 1987

**Kyle Howell**
b: 06 Jan 1987

**Gabriel Allen Davis**
b: 01 Sep 2009

**Craig Seigle Jr**
b: 10 Jun 2012

# PREFACE

I am Leslie John Kessler Junior; born October 3, 1923, to Leslie John Kessler Senior, and Rhoda Marie (Hyatt) Kessler. I've written this book, an account of many of the events of my life's journey, in an effort to record the story of God's hand in my life from my earliest memories to this present day. Some writers record the events of their lives to tell about the good things they have done. That is not my intention because there is nothing great about me. You see, I do not desire to give an account of why people love or admire me or why they don't. My purpose is to give God the glory and praise He deserves by sharing the events of my life including all the miracles He has allowed me to witness or participate in along the journey. I can now look back on every decade and see God's hand in the development of my life and how each step led to where I am now. To be doing what I am doing at the present time required some miracles from God: a certain nature, a born again Christian experience, knowledge of shipping, receiving, billing, sales, manufacturing, including the operation of many types of production machinery. It would also require a thorough knowledge of diamond products. It would require college and seminary degrees. I hope you will be inspired and encouraged as you read to look for the God thread in your own life because He has a divine purpose for each one of us.

I have wanted to write this book for many years, but procrastination, laziness, and fear of not being able to put it in the proper format kept me from doing so. My granddaughters, a golfing friend, my son, and many others ultimately eliminated all of my excuses. I would like to thank each of them from the bottom of my heart. Credit for this book goes first to my granddaughters who assured me they would help in any way they could. My son who gave me encouragement with his attitude of, "Go for it dad!" My wife who was always willing to back me in everything I felt led to do, simply said, "Kessler, if that is what you want to do, then do it." My golfing friend Alicia Jansen was instrumental in getting me started. Alicia is the daughter of another golfing friend named John Rounsap. John announced to me one day that he was bringing his daughter to play with us for the purpose of beating me soundly. She started playing regularly with us on Fridays. Alicia and I developed a great friendship, and she thoroughly enjoyed playing with her dad and his old buddies. Alicia and I have had a great friendly rivalry ever since. After golf one Friday, we were having lunch together, and I happened to mention my desire to write this book. She said, "Why don't you get started?" I gave her all my reasons, and she began to eliminate them one by one. She seemed very interested in some of the stories about weddings I had done. She, along with many others, inspired me to at least try to write this book. And finally to my wonderful editor Diahn Ehlers who turned a manuscript into a story.

Writing a book is much easier these days. I am told that you can always get someone to publish your manuscript. I remember that in years past, you had to have something that would sell millions of copies before anyone would publish the book. I understand now that with the advent of modern technology, most anyone can get a book published. This is a comforting truth because my family and friends may be the only ones to ever read this book.

# 1923-1933

# A Boy Named Leslie

A quick disclaimer before I begin. Many of the dates I will be citing in this book are "on or around about", historical accuracy being less important than the times their approximations indicate. That being said, I happened to be born on October 3, 1923, in Columbus, Texas. (This date is not approximate.)

When I was five years old, our family moved to Houston. Shortly thereafter, I developed double pneumonia and was near death. My father later told me, "Your mother and I had been advised by the doctor that you might not make it. We knelt by your bed and prayed that if God would spare your life, we would dedicate you to Him, and that night you began to recover." Our lives are greatly influenced by the things that happen around us whether or not we are aware of them.

But of the next incident, I was keenly aware. My father was packing to go somewhere (probably looking for another job). He put his loaded 38 revolver on the bed to be put in his suitcase with everything else he needed, and then went into the bathroom to shave. I walked into the bedroom at that exact moment, saw the gun, and picked it up to play Cowboys and Indians. I pointed the gun at numerous imagined foes all around the room. I think I even pointed it at myself in my excited enthusiasm. Mother was sitting at her dresser applying her makeup when I pointed the gun towards her and pulled the trigger. The bullet struck the end of our iron bed, was deflected, and fell to the floor. Had the bullet not ricocheted off the iron bed, it would have struck her in the back. I dropped the gun, and my father came running. Mother grabbed me. I was terrified. Dad sold the gun, and from that day forward, he never kept another gun in the house. I immediately acquired the utmost respect for guns, and never had one in my own home.

> Even after returning from WW II, I refused to keep a gun in my house. My advice to any parent that owns a gun is to keep it out of the reach of children, preferably in a locked gun cabinet. Pap-Paw

My father finally found work on a railroad project. It was hard labor, laying railroad tracks. The project was in Monahans, Texas, so we moved there in 1929. I was enrolled in public school for the first time, and I hated it. It seemed to me that all the other kids were smarter than I was. Mother was very patient with me, and did everything she could to help me get adjusted. Well, she *tried*, anyway.

No one in my family ever called me by my given name, Leslie. I was, from the very beginning and to my great disliking, Junior Kessler. Somehow though, I managed not to be referred to as Junior, but Leslie, at school. Probably because it showed up on the roll like that and no one in my family was around to "correct" the teacher. Being called by my given name was not without some complication, however. Leslie is a girl's name, and being a boy with a girl's name meant I was teased a lot, and I resented being teased.

The jeers persisted even at my new school, Harrisburg Elementary, where I was enrolled after our family moved back to Houston. But this time, it had a little less to do with my 'girlie' name . . . My mother dressed me for school each day with much care. She wanted her little boy to be handsome, even though she did not have much to work with. She dressed me in knickers which were the adult style of the day. I don't know if I can adequately describe knickers, but to a boy of my age they were horrible. They were designed to blouse over the knee. I always had skinny legs, and knobby knees (you would call them "bird legs" today). They looked ridiculous on me—at least I thought they did. Mother would plaster my cowlick down, place a little wool cap on my head, and send me off to school. There were no school busses, but we lived close enough for me to walk the distance. That gave me time to toss the cap, and pull the knickers as far below my knees as possible. All the boys at school wore long pants and cotton, patterned shirts. You cannot imagine the ribbing I took. I tried to explain to Mother that the other boys did not dress as she was dressing me. She replied, "Well, they are not as pretty as you are either."

I finally saved enough money to buy myself a pair of denim pants. They laced up the back and were bell bottom. I also bought a pair of tennis shoes ("tinny" shoes we called them). I guess my message finally hit home with my mother, and was I ever glad. She made me some short sleeved shirts out of terrycloth towels. When she observed my new attire, she finally admitted that her little boy looked a lot better. My terrycloth shirts were the envy of the boys in school, and they all wanted to know where I bought them. I said, "My mother made them, and she will not make any more."

## Opportunity Knocks

The Great Depression was a severe, worldwide economic depression in the decade preceding World War II. The timing of the Great Depression varied across nations, but in most countries it started in 1930 and lasted until the late 1930s or middle 1940s. It was the longest, most widespread, and deepest depression of the 20th century. Wikipedia

Life was very, very hard. There were very few jobs, and it was obvious to me, even at a young age, that my parents and their friends were extremely worried. If you listened in class or read history books, I am sure you have heard of this period in American history.

A few pennies went a long way in those days. You could buy one pound of bologna or a loaf of bread for just five cents. Prices were at rock bottom, and yet only a few people could afford meat, bread, milk and potatoes. This depression affected everyone. It was an equalizer, so to speak. Most of the rich had lost all their money, and the poor were still poor or even poorer. All Americans were in the same predicament—in the same soup lines that were everywhere. People and their families would wrap the buildings hoping the free soup wouldn't run out before they got to the front of the line, but it always did. Mother had to be very frugal. It is amazing how far a housewife can make food go when she has to.

A strong work ethic is something that is developed and does not come naturally. But hard times present many opportunities to someone who's looking, and I was constantly on the lookout. I found a small metal wagon and repaired it the best I could, and then toured the neighborhood picking up scrap metal. As soon as I filled the wagon, which usually took about a week, I would take it to the junk yard and sell the scrap iron there. The junk yard manager took a liking to me. He could very easily have taken advantage of me, but instead, he taught me that some metal was worth more than others. I learned that scrap aluminum, brass, and copper brought more money than anything else, but all scrap metal was worth something. I began looking for old pots and pans. Someone else's junk became my treasure. I managed to obtain a decent amount of spending money in this manner.

Later on, I sold the Saturday Evening Post magazine door-to-door, my first part-time job. The magazine was published once weekly. I do not remember the price of the publication, but since the magazine was popular, I managed to sell enough to earn a small percentage of my sales.

> There would be many more 'open doors' and other jobs which I will cover in later chapters. Suffice it to say, my advice to young people is to make the most of the opportunities given to you and not to think yourself overqualified for any job. Pap-Paw

# Game On

Most of my young friends were poor like me; however, I had one very affluent friend named Milton Butler whose father owned a shipping company. Milton was a good friend, and we got along very well. Milton told me how bored he was with all his expensive toys and the ways he and his wealthy friends entertained themselves. He seemed to really enjoy hanging out with me and the other neighborhood boys.

War games were easy to invent; war strategy, on the other hand, required some thought. I came up with a brilliant idea during one of our clay ball fights. I borrowed—stole really—my mother's metal garbage can lid, (Plastic had not been invented, yet.) and used the lid as a "shield" to ward off the clay balls being thrown at me by my enemies. The sticky mud would slam into my shield and stay there until I could scrape it off and throw the balls back at the enemy. I made another great discovery. I cut a limber switch, and stuck a mud ball on the end and proceeded to attack in this manner. I was able to whip the limber switch in such a way that the bomb could be sent directly at my enemies with high velocity. I was known as a great warrior. Of course, these advantages did not last very long because my enemies would soon come up with some defense or alternate strategy.

And then there was "rubber guns". Everyone was charged with making his own weapons. First, a piece of scrap wood was shaped into the form of a gun. Then a clothes pin was strapped to the handle. For ammunition, we used automobile tire inner tubes—real rubber. The inner tubes were cut into strips about one quarter inch wide. We would tie a knot in the middle. One end would go into the clothes pin and then be stretched to the end of the gun. You then squeezed the clothes pin. The rubber band, once released, traveled about fifteen feet with enough velocity to reach the target, but not enough to hurt anyone. I designed a very special weapon for myself by strapping clothes pins all around so that it would act like a machine gun.

Boy to boy shootouts from ten feet were occasional events, but the most popular was team wars. Sides were chosen. Usually, there were four or five boys on each side (sometimes more), and then it was game on. As soon as someone was hit with a rubber band, they were "dead" and out of the game. The last boy standing was the winner. I was good at the game and won many times. The trick was to hide and then jump out at the enemy and shoot him. When my wealthy cousin came to see me from Galveston, the first thing he wanted to do was go head to head. By the time he went home, he was filthy dirty and his nice clothes in complete disarray. My aunt was not too happy with me when Walter returned home. Walter was very happy though, and I am sure he introduced his well-to-do friends at home to the game as well.

I remember one particular boy would constantly deny being hit. I became aggravated that he would never admit it. In one battle, I hid myself, and when he came around the corner, I put my rubber gun to his chest and pulled the trigger. The rubber band made a loud "splat", and he ran home crying. He was not hurt, but his mother acted like I had killed him. His mother came to tell my mother how awful her child was for doing this terrible thing to her son. I tried to explain that it was the only way I could get him to admit he was hit, but she still reprimanded me and gave me a pinch. Now, my mother could pinch like no other person. She would reach under my thigh, get a good supply of skin, and twist. Her pinches were far worse than a paddling.

Games were seasonal. I still do not know what determined the game of the season except for in the case of "sticks" which had to be played in fall and winter when the clay fields were nice and muddy. As can be guessed, the game of sticks was played with a carefully selected, pointed stick. The boys alternated throwing their sticks into the mud. The object of the game was to throw your stick, knock the other stick down, and then knock it away so the boy with the fallen stick had to chase it down. The boy had to return before you could throw your stick three more times into the mud. If the boy did not get back in time, you won. If he did, you lost. I don't know what the purpose of the game was, well, except that it was competitive and a chance to get dirty. And this made it a favorite among the boys in my neighborhood.

There was "tops" and "marbles". And "tin can shinny" where we put on roller skates, took our homemade hockey sticks, and dropped a can in the street. The object was to get the can past the enemy and across a predetermined line at each end of the street. Our games were highly competitive, and this one especially produced many bumps and bruises. We had no protective gear, and in the heat of battle, it was impossible to hit a tin can without also smacking an occasional shin or ankle.

> Please notice something really important here. These games required no special equipment, no meticulously groomed fields, and no expensive uniforms. It didn't take a lot of money to play, just a little imagination. And I guarantee, no more fun is had today than we had then.

## Family Matters

My mother and father seemed to never get along. They argued constantly. I hated it. On one occasion, my father slapped my mother and cursed her. On another occasion, my mother slapped my father and cursed him. Nothing seemed to be going right for them, and I became distressed to the point of staying silent most of the time. Usually, my silence was written off as being 'shy', but the truth was I was hurting. I knew that my mother and father loved me dearly, but that did not seem to stop their fussing. Individually, they were wonderful people. Together, they were a natural disaster. Much later in life, I would learn about relationships, and the blessings of being a peacemaker—but this was neither my time nor my place, no matter how much I yearned for peace.

In spite of their marital problems, we still had some enjoyable, if not notable, family activities. Dad had managed to get a beginning job at Sinclair refinery on a part-time basis, but we, like most families, still had to look for the cheapest forms of entertainment possible. Going to the park was always a good choice. We also managed to go to the movies about once a month. There were five movie theatres in downtown Houston at the time. The Ritz, the epitome of the poor man's movie theatre and the best value for your dollar, always showed a double feature, the news, previews of coming attractions, and a comedy.

One particular night at the Ritz is etched in my memory. It's humorous now, but seemed disastrous at the time. We ate a lot of pinto beans in those days because they were 'good wholesome food', and easily seasoned. We had just finished a big dinner of pinto beans, cornbread, and sliced onion. The meal is delicious, but as most people know, it comes with consequences. We were at the theatre, sitting together among a full house, and I began to pass gas (like I said, "consequences"). I could not help it. I was about to blow up.

I do not know how my father knew it was me, but he reached over my mother and squeezed my arm and said, "Will you please stop doing that? Everyone thinks it is me." It was embarrassing to him, and if I wasn't careful, that embarrassment would turn into anger. I asked for permission to go down to the front of the theatre where most of the kids sat. My father answered, "Yes!"

I detected the urgency in his voice and surmised that he was rather glad when I left. During the comedy, I became consumed with laughter, and since I had failed to use the restroom for fear of missing something, I leaked a little urine, and then I could not stop laughing or leaking. When the movie was over, I went back to my parents. I must have been an awful sight for them to behold. They put me between them in abnormal proximity, and we walked like that out of the theatre and all the way to the car.

Ah, the car . . . now that's another story. It was an old Chevrolet coupe with a rumble seat. I would have loved to ride in the rumble seat, but I had good reason not to—and it wasn't wet pants that prevented me. There was an ice cream store on the way home, and I knew I would need some time in the front seat to make my petition for a double dip ice cream cone. Understandably, my father was a frugal man. He had to be. He was trying to feed a family on next to nothing, and every penny counted. Nonetheless, I would begin my ride home by asking my father, "Daddy, can I have a double dip?"

The standard reply was always, "Absolutely not, do you think money grows on trees? You go to bed with the wants and wake up with the gimmies!"

I was persistent, and the closer our approach to the ice cream place, the more I begged.

My mother would then pipe in, "Why don't you stop and get him an ice cream you stingy old (censored)?"

My father would screech the brakes in front of the ice cream store, hand me a nickel, and say, "HERE, TAKE IT!"

I would purchase my ice cream, get back in the car, and lick the treat between sobs. My parents could not afford that ice cream cone or much else, but they sacrificed for me as loving parents do. I am sure my father thought, "I hope you enjoy that for all you have put us through to get it," but he never said it out loud.

> The passage of time makes it possible for us to laugh at ourselves!
> Pap-Paw

## For Better and For Worse

When I was 10 years old, we attended an old fashioned tent revival as a family. It was one of those sawdust type events that took place in a vacant lot and it was well attended. I remember the night so well. I was sitting with my mother and father in the back row. Sometime during the sermon, the preacher explained the way to salvation.

He said, "No matter who you are, man, woman, boy or girl, there comes a time when you need to make a decision for Jesus Christ."

I thought about that.

Then he said, "No matter who you are, should you die not having the Lord Jesus in your heart, you will end up in Hell. If you have Jesus in your heart when you die, you will go to Heaven, and you have a choice to make tonight. You can decide for Christ, or against Him. You cannot be neutral. He either is or He isn't. The choice is yours."

The preacher gave an altar call, and I felt something I had never felt before. I knew I needed to respond. I went forward, not sure exactly what I was supposed to do. I was asked to kneel, and he began to pray with me. He asked me if I would like to invite Jesus to come into my heart.

I said yes, and something happened that is hard to explain. I knew nothing about theological terms like "born again" or "saved", but I understood that I had just asked Jesus Christ to be my Lord and Savior, that his Holy Spirit dwelt in me at that very moment and best of all, he was never going to leave me. I felt excited and scared all at the same time. I returned to my seat as quick as I could without running and begged my father and mother, "Would you please go back down there with me? There is something you must to hear."

They both declined despite my pleas and persistence, though they seemed to approve of the decision I made that night.

Several weeks passed by, and someone advised my mother that I needed to be baptized; Broadway Baptist Church was recommended to her. The preacher there talked to me about my decision and explained New Testament baptism to me and his belief that being baptized was the first thing you should do after becoming a Christian. There were about twenty other kids doing the same thing, and we were baptized one after another. I was now a proud member of Broadway Baptist Church.

And I was also what I term now "a baby in Christ". I was a part of a community of believers, but because my parents didn't attend church, I didn't get to attend services. We had a Bible at home, but it was difficult to understand, and I very quickly became discouraged and stopped reading it. I had the tools, but I didn't know how to use them. I wasn't growing spiritually; I just lived like the rest of my friends who knew nothing about the Bible, church membership or Jesus.

My mother and father continued to have marital problems. My father came to me one day and said, "Son, your mother and I are getting a divorce, and you will be living with your mother. This does not mean I do not love you. Times are hard, but I have a job, and I will do the best I can to help you and your mother."

In those days, there was no mandatory child support. Things had to be worked out between couples. I am sure the court gave my father a figure he was supposed to pay, but in those uncertain times, a court document meant very little. The divorce was final.

---

I believe that this trauma was responsible for shaping much of my personality and character as a reconciler. To this day, I loathe fusses and feuds between people—adults and children alike. I detested when two school mates were mad at each other. I remember on several occasions trying to patch up arguments between friends of mine. I was not a coward, nor a pacifist. There were some altercations I could not evade, and had to defend myself. I usually got whipped. I just did not want to hurt anyone, and chose to avoid conflict whenever possible. I seemed to be developing a peacemaking philosophy without knowing the Biblical urgency for Christians to be peacemakers.

---

## Worldly Perspective

Even in my relatively sheltered environment, I was constantly in earshot of adults talking about the problems in Europe. Our president was Herbert Hoover, and it seemed he was not only unpopular, but that he was to blame for the depression. I didn't know who or what was the cause, so I just went along with what the adults were saying. It is amazing how much we trusted adults in those days. There were also constant warnings about the rise in popularity of a man named Hitler in Germany, and many felt that if this man ever came in to power, bad things would begin to happen everywhere. All this was way over my head, and I mostly just concentrated on surviving in my own little world.

At the close of this, my first decade, Franklin D. Roosevelt was elected president. His campaign speeches were dynamic, and I couldn't help but take notice, if only as to how it directly affected me and my family. Words like, "I am going to create jobs and put Americans to work doing something," and "I will put a chicken in every pot," resonated with the hunger growls in my stomach.

He did all that and began to pull us out of the depression. He started a program called "WPA" and sent men to work on dams and other public works projects. I had eight uncles without jobs living in tents that went to work under this program, and all were able to manage very well.

I have heard since that many people did not like him, but as far as I was concerned, FDR was the man who began to lift us out of the greatest depression ever known.

# 1933-1943

# Growing Pains

I got my first paddling at Deady Junior High School. One day in my homeroom class, I was busily engaged in drawing an unflattering caricature of a classmate two rows over while my homeroom teacher, Mrs. Reynolds, watched with great stealth over my shoulder. I jumped when she suddenly asked, "Are you through, Leslie?"

After confiscating my art work, she sent a note home informing my parents that I was caught drawing obscene pictures. I don't remember the full extent of the disciplinary action, but a few things remain painfully clear. Like the pinch from my mother. And the promises to never draw anything like that again. Then there was the long walk down the empty halls to the principal's office.

> In those days, children could be punished by the school as the administrators saw fit; it was called corporal punishment.

Our principal had a paddle in his office, and as I walked through the opened door, I saw my basketball coach holding it across his lap. My heart fell; Coach was the last person I wanted to see. Not only was he a large man with an imposing grip, but I surmised that he would also take it out on me on the court in practice. Having just recently made the team, not knowing how this would affect my relationship with him made it even worse. Coach applied three strokes with the paddle as I bent over the principal's desk, but he never told anyone on the team about the incident. I appreciated and respected him for that decision. He did, however, let me know, in no uncertain terms, how displeased he was with my graphic portrayal.

While playing on the school basketball team, I fell in love with Bobbie Maddox—one of our cheerleaders. I liked her very much, but

I lacked the wherewithal to tell her so. Apparently, she liked me as well and sent one of her girlfriends to break the ice. This gave me the courage I needed to ask her out. Going to the movies and holding hands was intoxicating. And then she invited me to go ice skating with her. I knew nothing about ice skating. I had never ice skated in my life, but the very idea of skating with her was so exciting that I learned to skate. Bobbie was athletic, graceful, and accomplished on the ice. During our time together at the rink, I managed to develop enough skill to be able to be her "dance skating" partner. Our relationship ended gradually with little drama, but my fondness of her remains to this day.

His name was G. C. Fredel; I don't know how to fully describe this friend of mine except that he had a big fat nose, and he was amazingly strong. He made a point to catch me off guard as often as possible and hit me with a stiff blow to my skinny arm when I wasn't looking. (Friends did this?) Boys in those days were always hitting each other for some reason or no reason at all. I spent an equal amount of time trying to figure out some way to get even with him. G.C.'s seat was in the back of the classroom, and mine was in the front. One day, as I was walking toward my seat, I was hit with a sudden and compelling inspiration. I reached underneath his big fat nose and thumped, releasing the pressure between my thumb and my middle finger as hard as I could. It was not difficult to imagine the surprise and pain that resulted given the loud bellow that followed and the vow to beat me up after class. He kept mouthing to me, "I'm going to get you," whenever the teacher turned her back. I was lighter and faster than G. C., and he didn't catch me until the day he forgave me with a well-placed knee to my leg, a customary act of vengeance in those days. It hurt, but then we went on with our friendship.

## The Company You Keep

Milby High School had lots of character and lots of "characters" as students. One such group of kids called themselves "The Dead End Gang". I think they adopted the name after seeing a Hollywood movie with the same title. They were tough when they traveled together, but not much individually. I steered clear of them as much as I could after observing several bruised and battered faces of guys who crossed their path. It did not take much to have them after you. School authorities took little notice, but several of them got in trouble with the law. One kid was eventually shot down and killed on his street by the police. His death seemed to calm the rest of the gang down a little bit.

I only had a couple of close friends, and I considered Carl Jarvis one. He watched over me with a brotherly protectiveness. Carl was about one year older than I and much more mature. He was very wise for his years, an excellent student, and a great athlete. He was especially good at boxing, and regularly entered the Golden Gloves boxing tournaments and once won the city championship in his welter weight division. He did not go any further because his family could not afford the traveling expenses. It was through Carl and by him that I encountered my first "what goes around comes around" experience.

A group of us were together at a carnival on South Main Street. We had no money to spend on the rides, but we liked to watch patrons as they paid their quarter, entered the ride, were strapped in and elevated and then maneuvered their plane. Someone (Carl!) decided it would be great fun to play a prank on one of the riders—oil of mustard immediately came to mind. Carl worked at a drug store part-time; therefore, he was volunteered for the task of obtaining (confiscating) the oil. A small amount of the substance would be put in a capsule, and one of us would carry it up in the ride. When the ride was finished, the perpetrator would place the oil of mustard on the seat. The unsuspecting person to go up next would be strapped in as the mustard oil made contact with his skin and began a slow burn. By the time the "victim" was able to disembark, his bottom would be on fire! The plan took several days to implement and by go-time, we managed to pool enough money for one of us to ride. Carl insisted that since he was going to be a future flyer and had provided the oil of mustard, he was the logical choice and we agreed.

Carl boarded the plane with the capsule hidden deep in his back pocket and a sly smile on his face. Then a strange thing happened. When the ride was finished, instead of completing the plan as we so eagerly anticipated, Carl bolted out of his seat as soon as he was unstrapped and took off running.

We yelled after him, "Hey Carl, where are you going?"

He neither answered nor slowed down in his rush toward the filling station across the street. We followed and found him sitting in the sink soaking his backside! Apparently, the oil of mustard capsule in Carl's back pocket drained out in his own seat. He was strapped in and we could not hear him hollering. He threatened us with violence if we laughed, but I couldn't help it. It cracked me up. What a lesson we learned that day.

I dated quite a few girls after Bobbie Maddox. Though some were interesting, most were unremarkable. Let's just say that I liked girls, a lot, but the way June Hale made me feel was altogether DIFFERENTT. The first time I saw her, I was walking with a friend of mine, and June and her cousin Tiny (she wasn't small) were walking from the opposite direction. June had a corncob pipe in her mouth.

I thought to myself, "How odd, but my, how pretty."

The next week, I saw June coming down the same sidewalk. This time she had a cigar in her mouth! I, once again, thought this was very strange, and decided that there must be something wrong with her. However, I found her both attractive and intriguing and couldn't seem to get the thought of her out of my mind.

June graduated from Edison Junior High School in the following weeks and showed up on Milby's campus. I was in my sophomore year and she was a freshman when we were finally introduced.

> She would never admit it for fear of seeming "forward", but I'm convinced that she instigated the meeting and was the first to suggest that we go out together.

After only one date, we became inseparable and declared to all our friends that we were going steady.

> Going steady/dating /going out / boyfriend and girlfriend—you get the picture!

Eventually, curiosity got the best of me and I just had to ask, "When I saw you the first time you had a corn cob pipe in your mouth, and the next time I saw you with a cigar. What was that all about?"

She casually replied, "Tiny dared me to do it, so I did. I do not smoke!"

## Making it Work

Money was still scarce, so our dates were simple; June and I just wanted to be with each other as much as we could. At that time, I worked at Glenbrook Golf Course on Saturdays. I would show up early and try to go out as a caddie; there were many more caddies than golfers. Sometimes I was successful, and sometimes I was not. When successful, I made seventy-five cents for eighteen holes of golf. A good tip was ten cents. You could expect a tip provided you did not lose any of the golfer's balls and catered to his whims. It felt like the golf bag weighed as much as I did. This kind of job was not going to provide me with what I needed, so I put my name on a long waiting list for a Houston Press paper route.

After waiting in line for a year, I finally got the paper route. Now I had a little money, but not much. A lot of it went towards helping my mother with rent and food. June would often save her lunch money (twenty five cents) and we would go out to a place on Harrisburg Boulevard that sold barbeque sandwiches-two for fifteen cents. That left ten cents for two sodas. We chose the larger, sixteen full ounce drinks such as R C Cola, Root Beer, and Pepsi Cola. We enjoyed attending park dances and taking long walks at Mason Park, just being together was enough for us. After saving up for quite a while, I managed to buy an old 1934 Ford that would barely run, but it was transportation and enabled us to venture further on our outings. There was a drawback, however; a typical trip of twenty-five miles, more times than not, required the fixing of at least one flat tire.

## God Speed

We discovered ourselves to be very much in love and made the commitment to get married someday. That day was to come sooner rather than later; the Japanese bombed Pearl Harbor on December 7, 1941 triggering the beginning of World War II. As a result, I left Milby High School in the middle of my senior year lacking only one subject credit to graduate: Civics, which thankfully, held no interest for me at the time. I immediately went to work for the Ordinance Depot.

> The Ordinance Depot was built solely for the purpose of storing weapons and munitions after America was compelled to enter the war.

Fortunately, I made enough money for June and I to talk seriously about marriage and our immediate future. It was inevitable that I would at some point be called into military service, and neither of us could live with the uncertainty of waiting until the war was over. Our parents were willing to sign the necessary papers required for us to wed, and June and I were married on Christmas Eve, 1941. Eleven months later, Ronald David was born.

> The birth of our son was a blessed event in our lives; however, June had a hard time with labor and decided she did not want any more children.

Shortly thereafter, I left the Ordinance Depot and went to work for Hughes Tool Company. It was at Hughes Tool that I met a man named Marshall Hayes in the Engineering Department while I was charged with operating a production grinding machine. Marshall's job was to evaluate grinding wheels. He was required to have a thorough knowledge of abrasives. He chose me to run the tests for him, and we developed a great friendship.

I received notice from the Draft Board that I was to take a physical and then be classified for the draft; Ronnie was only six months old. All my friends assured me saying, "Don't worry, you are too skinny. They are not going to draft you." The following week I received my classification: One A. The next day I received an induction notice that I had been selected for military service and was to report to Fort Sam Houston in San Antonio, Texas. It was late in the evening, and all my immediate family was there. Many of them were crying while saying their goodbyes. I embraced my wife, son, mother, and my father and wondered deep in my heart when or if I would ever see them again. I boarded the train with hundreds of fellow inductees.

I was gravely concerned that June would be hard pressed for money. We had been told that wives would receive seventy-five dollars per month from the government and that my pay would be twenty-three dollars per month. I was so worried. Many men in my situation were given discharges because of family obligations. I praise God still today for my mother-in-law and my mother. They took care of my wife and baby for me while I couldn't. Without them, my family would not have survived.

> My mother-in-law loved me dearly and her name for me was "Son"; my mother always referred to me as "Babe". I will be forever grateful for their help during this time.

I arrived at Fort Sam and was inducted into the Army in 1942. I was then sent to Fort Belvoir, Virginia, for combat engineer basic training. America had to get ready for war in a hurry; basic training was condensed to a six week program. Training put weight on the thin fellows and took weight off of the heavy ones. I began to put on weight and muscle. We were all so young. I was the only one of my group that was married, and I took pride in showing the guys pictures of June and Ronnie. The hot summer was almost unbearable. The hardest training for me was the long hikes with full field packs while on water discipline. I learned a few tricks when on water discipline, though. I kept a lemon in my jacket and would occasionally sneak a suck. When a piece of fruit was not available, I used a small, smooth rock which would produce a little saliva in my mouth and enable me to swallow.

After completing basic training, I was sent to Staten Island, New York, Automobile Mechanics School for three months. I was instructed in maintaining military equipment. These were lonely months, but I enjoyed the few visits to Times Square in New York City. I rode a ferry to get there and passed right by the Statue of Liberty. What a beautiful sight! The Paramount Theatre was the hot spot for young people; top celebrity performances and first run movies were a big hit. I had often heard that New Yorkers were unfriendly, but I found them to be just the opposite, especially in regards to us servicemen.

For example, it was well publicized that Frank Sinatra was going to be at the Paramount Theatre. When I got there, the line was so long that if you were at the end there was no guarantee you could even get a seat. I headed for the back of the line, but the patrons in front of me insisted, "No soldier, you go to the front of the line."

An usher standing outside the theatre came and got me and took me directly to the cashier. I was charged only the tax, everything else was free. Frank Sinatra took the stage and sang "All or Nothing at All". Girls were screaming and fainting on every aisle. This was the first time I had witnessed females being overcome by a song to the point of collapsing—it was quite a sight.

After completing the three months program at Staten Island, I was sent to Fort Ord, California, and assigned to Company C of the 593$^{rd}$ Engineer and Boat Regiment. I now weighed 165 pounds and was in the best physical condition of my life. The 593$^{rd}$ was training for operating landing craft for beachhead landings of troops and supplies. The war could not be won without such craft. Ours was an

Army unit. There was also a Navy unit with the same shoulder patch as ours, except theirs was red and ours was blue.

> The craft we would be using was specially designed by Wiggins Boat Company in New Orleans, Louisiana, at the urging of the United States Government: LCM, landing craft mechanized, designed to land troops, tanks, trucks, and carry supplies. The craft was very sturdy. The ramp in front could be raised or lowered, depending on the need. The LCM had twin screws (propellers), and twin GMC diesel engines. Higgins Company worked three shifts, seven days a week, trying to fill the government's requirements and hired mostly women because the majority of men were being drafted into military service.

Company C received their orders, and we were loaded onto a troop ship and taken out under the Golden Gate Bridge. We did not know where we were going, but the scuttlebutt was that we were headed for the South Pacific.

> Scuttlebutt—a navy term for rumors or gossip passed among service men. "Word on the street"

I stood on the stern of that troop ship and watched the Golden Gate Bridge until it faded completely out of sight. Oh, how the pangs of loneliness overwhelmed me as I watched what I knew of family, home, and country fade into the distance having no idea what lay ahead for me.

We arrived in the South Pacific and landed on Goodenough Island near New Guinea during a heavy rain. Our landing crafts were still on the way, and were not scheduled to arrive for two weeks. There were no enemy troops on the island. This was simply a station for us to get ready. For the next two weeks we were put on jungle detail, cutting down trees with cross cut saws (what I would have given for a nonexistent chain saw!) to be used for building a station and field hospital on the island. Our landing craft arrived, and I was assigned to First Platoon, Boat C. The crafts had three or four man crews consisting of coxswain, engineer, deck hand and a machine gunner. Most of our craft's deck hands were also supposed to be the machine gunner. I was the engineer. My coxswain was Don Larson, and the deck hand was Chester Sullivan. Later, we all cross trained: I could operate the craft as well as the coxswain, and the deck hand knew much about engineering. This versatility would soon become critical to our survival.

# 1943-1953

# Wars-with-in-War

We were assigned to an Australian Division whose commands were to make landings with troops, tanks, and supplies to all the beachheads being established there. I came to admire the Australian men we worked under; they were fair minded, rugged individuals with great jungle-fighting skills. They wore large, wide brimmed hats with chin straps that were excellent for blocking the sun's rays, and their outer clothing was ideal for withstanding the humidity of the tropics. The more time we spent in their company, the more accustomed we became to their speech and the closer we came to understanding the meaning of their words. At times, you could even catch us mimicking our new comrades just for the fun of it. Not one person ever took offense.

> Landings are invasions; Beachheads are the establishment and headquarters for the invasion. These are amphibious terms.

It was the Australian servicemen who first introduced us to the New Guinea Aborigines. These indigenous people had no formal education, but were wise to the jungle and all of its elements, pulling from it everything from food and shelter to clothing and defense. That is, until they were given access to the razor blades that the Australians brought to trade for fresh bananas. It's hard to imagine how they groomed themselves before then. Sometimes the Aborigines would join the work parties on our craft. To our misfortune, the wheel house happened to be behind the well deck where the group of men stood for the duration of the trip. The ever constant sea breeze kept everyone reasonably comfortable, but it also carried the crowd's strong body odor straight back to me and my crew.

We began to make landings up and down the coast of New Guinea in Bogjim, Madang, Alexishafen, Hollandia, Aitape, and Borneo. Pulling up to the beach in the heavy surf of the South Pacific was terrifying. The giant waves may have created a surfer's paradise, but for us, they conjured up a nightmarish predicament. Many times, as we navigated our craft toward the sand loaded with troops or tanks, we would get caught up in one of the gigantic swells, and it would slam us onto the beach. When the water rushed back to the ocean, it left us high and dry. Before the troops had time to gather their wits and completely vacate the craft, bulldozers already stationed on the beach would hurriedly push us back into the water with the hope of providing us with an opportunity to back out of harm's way. I was thankful that I could retreat in relative safety, but my heart ached as the soldiers disembarked. I knew that many of those courageous men charging the enemy beaches would not return alive. It never got easier for me to watch them go.

> Just how serious a menace malaria could be was shown when Dr. H. Y. Evatt, Australian Minister for External Affairs, revealed that more than 80 per cent of the Allied forces in New Guinea were attacked by malaria. In the first Burma campaigns, up to 85 per cent of the men suffered from malaria. By 1944, the position was very different. Malaria remained a great menace, but the armies had come to grips with it, and a great degree of control had been achieved.

But then, nothing about this time was easy. Biting mosquitos were so thick in areas that sometimes it was impossible to breathe without inhaling a mouthful of them. And they were tenacious little suckers. As a result and despite my faithful use of the preventive medicine Atabrine, I was infected with the worst of the jungle fevers: mosquito-borne malaria. My symptoms came and went at different intensities and for different lengths of time, but one particularly painful episode, fraught with fatigue and vomiting, sent me to the Australian field hospital for about three weeks. Here, patients with gunshot wounds, jungle fevers, shell shock and other problems all shared the same space. Lying in the bed next to me was an American soldier who looked to be about the same age as me. He didn't seem to have physical injuries, so I wondered why he was there.

He asked me one day, "What are you here for?"

"Malaria," I replied.

He responded, "That must be what is wrong with me."

I can't explain why, but talking to him made me realize that something was definitely wrong. I guessed that he was probably "shell shocked"—that the trauma of warfare had caused him to disconnect from reality. During one of our conversations, I learned that several weeks beforehand, he had received a letter from his fiancée; it was a "Dear John"; a break up letter. He asked me to read it. The words in that letter were careless and cruel, and I agonized over the fact that apparently, absence did not always make the heart grow fonder.

How could anyone do this to a soldier overseas?

It wasn't the first time that I'd heard of this happening. These letters were being received by servicemen everywhere, but it was the first time I'd been this close to the destruction it caused. I knew deep down that June would never do that to me, and I was more grateful than ever that she was my wife. The soldier's mental problems must have worsened while he was there. The last I saw, this poor soul was being escorted from the hospital in a straitjacket.

While the exact origins of the phrase are unknown, it is commonly believed to have been coined by Americans during World War II. Large numbers of American troops were stationed overseas for many months or years, and as time passed many of their wives or girlfriends decided to begin a relationship with a new man rather than wait for the original one to return. As letters to servicemen from wives or girlfriends back home would typically contain affectionate language such as "Dear Johnny", "My dearest John", or simply "Darling", a serviceman receiving a note beginning with a curt "Dear John" would instantly be aware of the letter's purpose. A writer in the Democrat and Chronicle of Rochester, NY, summed it up in August 1945:

"Dear John," the letter began. "I have found someone else whom I think the world of. I think the only way out is for us to get a divorce," it said. They usually began like that, those letters that told of infidelity on the part of the wives of servicemen . . . The men called them "Dear Johns".

Some bouts of malaria were harder for me to get over than others. The absolute worst episode occurred while we were in convoy to invade Borneo after having completed all the other landings in New Guinea. Our craft, along with close to fifteen others, had been loaded into a Navy LSD—Landing Ship Dry Dock. It was on this journey that my symptoms were severe enough to require immediate medical attention. The medical craft at the rear of the convoy was radioed and they instructed to drop me off on a small island along the way. The medical team would then stop, pick me up, and provide me with treatment. My crew dropped me off with a cot, a mosquito net, and a supply of canned rations. They pulled away, and a new wave of nausea caused me to double over. It was both a blessing and a curse that I couldn't watch them go—leaving me behind.

I'm not sure at what point I realized that the relief vessel had passed me by, but it wouldn't have mattered. I hadn't been provided with flares; I shouldn't have needed them. For the almost twenty-four hours that I was stranded, the very real possibility that I would die in that desolate place tortured me more than the cold sweat and throbbing headache that had landed me there. The medical ship did eventually retrieve me, and my symptoms were quite rapidly relieved, but the trauma of that experience took a really long time to shake.

On a more positive note, the Borneo landing was a success. We expected more intense resistance, but our planes had strafed the beaches thoroughly, and the Navy had launched rockets. Much damage had been done to the enemy forces before we even got there.

## The Shrinks

The Australians were having difficulty subduing the well trained Japanese jungle fighters and decided to enlist the help of the Dyaks. These savage people had practiced head hunting and shrinking as a religious ritual and form of warfare for decades. The process was both intriguing and repulsive. The next step after acquiring a person's head was to remove all the bone structure and the eyes. Then the eye lids and lips were sewn shut. So as to keep its shape, a perfectly round rock, slightly larger than a clinched fist, was inserted and the two sides of the opening were sewn together. The head was promptly soaked in some secret solution and then hung over a fire until it shrunk to about a fifth of its original size, still retaining its familiar facial features. Once the process was complete, the "shrinker" would hang his trophy at the front of his hut as proof of his prowess: the more shrunken heads, the greater the warrior.

A Dyak warrior used only one weapon, his sword. The swords were specifically forged and designed for one purpose—to separate an enemy's head from his body. These mercenaries moved so swiftly and silently in the jungle that many a Japanese soldier, as skilled as he was, lost his head before he knew what hit him. As an incentive, the Aussies offered the Dyaks a case of corned beef for every Japanese soldier they killed. To prove their kills, they brought the severed heads to the Aussies, who quickly informed them that physical proof was unnecessary and that an honest head count would suffice.

I found myself in the company of the Dyak people only when my boat carried an Australian patrol up one of the many rivers in their territory. On such occasions, my crew would tie up at the pier adjacent to and farthest away from the Australian and Dyak camps. None of us ever felt safe at such close proximity, and my crew and I took turns on lookout duty—on high alert at all times. I was especially uncomfortable because, in those days, I had a full head of dark, wavy hair, and I sensed that sometimes they gazed too intently—longingly, even—at my head. I made certain that I was near at least one Australian soldier at all times.

In a chance meeting, I was introduced to the Dyak chief and was awed by his uniquely crafted sword and scabbard—complete with decorative human hair. As difficult as communication was, I managed to express my desire to make a trade for it. After much hand gesturing, we reached a mutual agreement: a rusty, but functional shotgun I had found on one of our landings for his sword. I think we both considered ourselves shrewd for having gotten the better of the other guy. The chief replaced the human hair with goat's hair, at my request, and the sword now hangs prominently in my office.

I have had the joy and honor of showing this treasure in two of my great grandchildren's fifth grade classes as part of their study of the Pacific war.

For more in depth coverage of the relationship between my Army Amphibian Brigade and The Australian Army's efforts in liberating Borneo, look for a book entitled, "Operation Borneo", by Case and Pounds. It is being made available by First Books Publishing Company, 1663 Liberty Drive, Suite 200, Bloomington, Indiana, 47403.

## Over, But Not Done

The war ended shortly after the liberating of Borneo. We received the news late one afternoon, and I could hardly believe my ears. At the time, my craft and three others were anchored together in the harbor. A sister craft motored by as fast as it could go—the men on board shouting at the top of their voice, 'THE WAR IS OVER! THE JAPANESE HAVE SURRENDERED!"

Were they drunk? Playing a really bad trick on us? We were unsure and hesitant to get our hopes up until the formal announcement came the following day. Even then, it felt surreal and it was hard to believe that we were being asked to begin turning in our weapons. But since we were given orders to do just that, we anticipated with enthusiasm that it must mean we would be going home immediately.

While still anchored together in the harbor a week later and now without protection, we heard gun fire at close range. We were informed that the Japanese on the island had refused to surrender, had slipped through the Australian lines, and were now in the center of our camp. It was a suicide mission; these men wanted to die fighting. We were urged to stay where we were (I happily obliged) until a "mop-up" operation could be initiated. The scattered remnants of the beaten Japanese forces were going to be cleared out or rounded up. At sun-up the next morning, our shore battalion united with the Australians. Every one of those Japanese soldiers perished in the clash, quelling the attack.

## Patience Boys!

We were more than ready to go home. But the shipping industry was experiencing a workers' strike, and there were no direct routes back to the States. It took two months to secure transportation to the Philippines where we set up camp and began the waiting period for a troop ship home. Fortunately, the atmosphere in camp was relatively tranquil. We spent our leisure time playing volleyball, basketball, and ping pong. We were also offered a two-day pass to Manila, and most of us went, including me.

While on leave, a civilian rushed me from behind and had raised a six inch blade to stab me in the back. He would have been successful if a Navy sailor had not seen it coming and thwarted the attack. I couldn't fathom why that man had wanted to kill me, but I had no desire to ever go back to Manila. Stories of Americans being killed by Filipinos began to circulate. I just could not understand. America had liberated this country. Why were we so hated?

The troop ship we had waited for three months to get to us finally arrived, and we boarded for home. We landed at a port of debarkation in Oakland, California, and were immediately placed under quarantine—for six weeks. The experience wasn't that bad; the worst of it was by our own doing. The food we were served was delicious, and we were given whatever we wanted to eat and as much of it as we could hold. Needless to say, we couldn't "hold" much. None of us were used to rich foods at first, and the quantity we consumed caused everyone, including me, great misery. Thankfully, our bodies adjusted rather quickly, and we made it a priority to make up for lost time—we ate like pigs.

After the quarantine period had passed, I was allowed to go on liberty to Oakland. I chose to go on Christmas Eve, my wedding anniversary, so that I could call June. Oh, how I longed to hear her voice and to wish her a Happy Anniversary! But I could not find a working phone anywhere: the strikes had shut down virtually all service companies. I returned to camp more miserable than I had been at any point before. I was stuck, and all I could do was wait for my discharge orders.

"If they'd just turn me loose, I'd get home. I'll walk if I have to!"

Two weeks later, I boarded a troop train bound for Fort Sam Houston in San Antonio, Texas. The trip took three days. There was no running water for a bath, and we had no clean clothes to change into. As soon as I arrived, I was formally discharged from the Army, called June and my family to advise them of my estimated time of arrival, and then quickly boarded a Greyhound bus headed for Houston—the last leg of my long journey. The four hour trip felt like an eternity. The bus must have stopped at every small town along the way. The only thing that kept me from losing it was visualizing how June and Ronnie and my parents and mother-in-law might look after all this time.

My entire family met me at the bus station. I could see them through the bus window before they could see me—they looked absolutely wonderful! My heart pounded so hard it felt like it would burst out of my chest. As soon as I stepped off the last step, my three and a half year old son broke free from his mother and ran headlong into my outstretched arms. He recognized me from seeing the pictures I had sent home as often as possible. June had also made a point of reading Ronnie all my letters, telling him where I was at any given time, and making it all seem like a grand adventure. For just a brief moment, the face of the devastated soldier in the field hospital flashed through my mind, and a wave of exhaustion poured over me, but as soon as I kissed June—for the first time in two years—the image faded and in its place were elation and overwhelming thankfulness.

## Money Matters

I was discharged with $500 dollars in my pocket. That was more money than I had ever had at any given time, and I had big plans for it. First, I was going to take it easy for about a month—enjoy my family, catch up with old friends, sleep until noon. Next, I was going to purchase an entirely new wardrobe. I had left home weighing 129 pounds and came back weighing 165 pounds. Not only was I heavier, but all my proportions had changed, too. Then, I would buy us a good used car. What a thrill it was going to be to have our own transportation and not have to ride the bus all the time! My $500 did not last more than a day. I was responsible for paying a $200 grocery bill, a $200 phone bill—run up by June's intoxicated aunt—and several smaller bills that had accumulated while I was away.

I desperately needed a steady paycheck, and quick. I was able to land several small, manual labor jobs fairly easily, but attacks of malaria made it difficult to perform that type of physical work consistently enough for me to be able to provide for my family.

Full-time jobs were very scarce; you almost had to know someone in a company just to get an interview. Thankfully, my father was able to come through for me on this front. He knew someone at the new Goodyear rubber plant being built in Pasadena, and he encouraged me to apply.

"I hear they are hiring and that three hundred jobs are being made available. I have a contact on the inside. All you have to do is get an interview and my buddy will see that you get hired".

This was exactly the break I needed. I hurried to the Goodyear employment office and filled out an application. There were at least six hundred other people doing the exact same thing. We were all given tests, and I figured that a decent effort on my part, along with my father's good word, would seal the deal. The list of results was posted on the testing room door, and it took several minutes for me to get close enough to see mine. The top 300 were granted interviews—I was not among them. I realized at that moment how foolish I had been for dropping out of high school.

After several weeks of rejections, I decided to throw myself on the mercy of Hughes Tool. I thought it would work in my favor, so I told the gal in the personnel office that I was an employee before going into the service. She pulled my record and found that I had actually quit. I admitted and apologized for my intent to deceive her—I was just so desperate to be able to work and take care of my family. She must have understood my dilemma and done a good job explaining it to the guy in charge of new hires, because he agreed to see me.

He told me, "I appreciate your honesty. We need people like you. I'll just change your record to say you left for military service, which will entitle you to your job back, plus all seniority accumulated during the war which will allow you to choose your own shift."

It was an answer to prayer! While I had been looking for employment, I had also enrolled at the University of Houston taking advantage of the GI Bill that granted government assistance to veterans seeking a degree. The program took care of my tuition, books and supplies. Being able to make my own schedule at Hughes meant that I could work and go to school at the same time. I could barely maintain my composure long enough to shake the man's hand, say thank you and sprint home to tell June. I rushed out of his office and ran through the front door of my house. I am certain that the neighbors could hear the cheers.

While at Hughes, I earned an Associate of Science degree, received a promotion, moved into the engineering department, and became an assistant to my friend Marshall Hayes in charge of testing diamond products. I had held that position for three years when one of our diamond suppliers, J.K. Smit and Sons, expressed their need for a representative in Texas. On Marshall's recommendation, I interviewed and was very impressed that a company car, an expense account, and a credit card came with the job. I was by no means an experienced sales man, but I eagerly accepted the offer. I had been at Hughes Tool for a long time and knew my job well, but now I was out of my element. On more than one occasion, I went to pick up the phone to call my old boss and ask for my job back, but I stuck it out, and while I was not the top salesman at J. K. Smit, I was not the worst either.

Eventually, Marshall also left Hughes and went into partnership with my competitor. He offered me a position and I was very interested in, but his partner and he didn't see eye to eye, and I was not given the job. I have to admit that I was confused and angered by how the whole thing went down, but it was not something I had control over and the best thing for me to do was to let it go.

## Home Sweet Home

Family life was uncomplicated. My son was an absolute delight, my parents and in-laws were enjoyable. My beautiful wife was a great cook, and we were very much in love. During the work week, I looked forward to the good wholesome meal June would have already on the table when I got home, and I made great effort to be on time to eat it. She was also a meticulous housewife. Create a mess in her house, and she would be up in arms.

> I have since come to realize just what an effort June put forth; the toughest job in the world is that of a full time housewife with children.

June and I enjoyed spending time together feeding the ducks at the park, playing with Ronnie, and listening to radio programs like "The Shadow" and "The Red Skelton Show"—we didn't own a television.

> Full-scale commercial television broadcasting did not begin in the United States until 1947. The number of television sets in use rose from 6,000 in 1946 to some 12 million by 1951. No new invention entered American homes faster than black and white television sets. By 1955 half of all U.S. homes had one. History of Television, Grolier Encyclopedia, Article by Mitchell Stephens

But most of all, I loved to slow dance with my wife. Gliding across the dance floor with her in my arms took no effort at all. Put "Moonlight Serenade" by Glenn Miller or "Stardust" by Artie Shaw on the juke box, and we were in heaven—or at least I was. Although I wasn't any good, June could always talk me into joining her for the "jitterbug" or "swing". Ronnie would stand on a chair so he could watch us with a huge grin on his face.

June and I went from a one bedroom apartment with rent at less than $30 a month to our first new home thanks to the GI Bill. Under this bill, we could buy the house with no down payment and for $53 dollars a month. It was a two bedroom, one bath, with a carport in Jacinto City—a new community just outside Houston city limits. The total price was $3,500 dollars. It was going to stretch our budget a little thin, but we moved into our new home in 1950. Of course June decided we also needed new furniture, so we purchased what we "needed" from Sears on their installment plan.

## Boys Will Be Boys

As often as possible, I would hurry home after work to join Ronnie and the children that lived on our block for a game. On one such evening, I arrived to find a street football game already in progress. As soon as he saw me, my son came running up to me all excited that he had made up the rules, chosen the teams, and now his side was winning by sixty points! I was barely able to suppress my laughter, but I managed to reply with an appropriately stern voice.

"It's no wonder, Son. You made up the rules and you picked the teams—you have the whole game balanced in your favor." Despite the rebuke for his tactics, he listened while I proceeded to teach the entire group how to properly balance the teams and make the rules fair for both sides. Although he looked embarrassed, I think he felt good that his dad was out there. The other dads, in general, weren't known to take time to get involved.

There never seemed to be enough of it, but my time with my son was something I cherished. As I was watching Ronnie play with his basketball one Saturday morning at the park, several much larger boys ran up and stole it away from him. I went over and spoke to them calmly, but the largest boy seemed reluctant to return the ball to its rightful owner.

"You're not my daddy, you can't give me orders."

"No," I said, "I am not your father. I am this boy's father, and that is why I am taking *his* ball from *you* and giving it back to *him*."

I snatched the ball out of the bully's hands and gave it back to Ronnie. He was scared, but I think he knew I was protecting him.

Much to my relief, our father-son bond was deepening despite my early absence. I took Ronnie with me to the men's room while we were out one afternoon, and we were sharing the same toilet. There happened to be a roach in the bowl that was desperately trying to crawl out. We caught him in crossfire, knocking him back down every time he tried to crawl out. Fortunately for the roach, we ran out of ammunition before he drowned. The story still makes both of us laugh.

## Encroaching Darkness

Sharing the normal, uncomplicated joys of life with my wife and my son helped me shut out most of the horrors of World War II—but I wasn't always successful in my attempts. On many nights, I had trouble sleeping. I was often introverted, prone to mood swings, and distrustful of almost everyone.

When America went to war with North Korea, the military tried desperately to entice the well-trained veterans of WWII back into commission. They went so far as to offer double time since the date of discharge and for the time spent overseas. I was not tempted at all; I had experienced my fair share of war and was already coping with the after effects—the lingering malaria that was painfully slow in leaving my system being just part of it. The threat of Communism was menacing, and many otherwise confident Americans were building fallout shelters in their back yards. Trusted allies were now sworn enemies. The conflict was hard for me to understand. The resultant stress and uncertainty triggered flash backs of mutilated bodies and tortured soldiers. It was a dark time for me. I found little relief for my pain and fear; the occasional social cocktail began to turn into a compulsive daily routine.

**Dyak Warriors**

**Dyak Chief**

**LCM Craft Crewman with Dyak Warriors**

# 1953-1963

## Where is your heart?

June and I were drinking too much. And I traveled a lot for work. We no longer went dancing; the joy of the juke box had totally evaporated, and the atmosphere had long since stopped being healthy for a child. Ronnie was now a teen, anyway, and had his own set of friends and things to do. June and I hung out in local taverns most every night—together, but not really. My wife showed no interest in me and preferred her friends' company to mine. Who could blame her? They were there for her all those times that I was not.

I traveled more days during the week than I was home, and as a traveling salesman, it was easy for me to find companionship on the road. I am not sure when I first decided that I had good cause to be unfaithful, but somewhere along the line, I forgot the promises I had made to June on our wedding day. Instead of providing me a respite from loneliness, my actions made me completely miserable. I felt guilty all the time. Although neither of us had brought it up yet, divorce seemed imminent.

> "You are never a great man when you have more mind than heart."
> **Beauchene**

It was 1955, and I was making a business trip to Tulsa, Oklahoma. I checked into my hotel room, went out and had dinner, and returned to my room. Television was of no interest to me. I was too worried and soul sick. I decided to just go to bed. I looked around the room for something to read, and usually there were ample supplies of magazines, but this time the only thing available was a Gideon Bible. I picked it up and opened it. I do not know what passage it opened to, but God spoke to me. Had anyone else been in the room they may not have heard it, however, I did.

The words were spoken directly to my soul, "My son, you know what you must do".

The memories of my salvation experience instantly flooded my mind. I wept, and confessed my sins to God—it took a while. The next day I flew home and confessed all my sins to my wife and asked her to forgive me. I told her about the religious experience, but I didn't share with her that I was a Christian. The look on her face told me that she thought I had gone crazy. She said she forgave me with her mouth, but in her heart, there were doubts. I knew it would take time to prove that I had reached a turning point in my life and that things would never be the same again.

The next Sunday I attended the First Baptist Church of Jacinto City. Dr. G. C. Hodge was pastor. At the end of the service, I went forward and told him my story. Dr. Hodge quizzed me about my profession of faith in Christ as a child and was convinced that I knew what I was doing. I knew perfectly well I had given my heart to Christ that night at the revival in 1933. Dr. Hodge seemed satisfied and asked me to dedicate the rest of my life to Christ. The church contacted my previous pastor and requested my membership letter. I was amazed and relieved that Broadway Baptist still had me on their church roll after all those years.

> Some churches cleanse their roll every so often, but I am a firm believer of the "once a member, always a member" policy. Everyone on the role needs prayer and intercession, and if they are lost, to be found.

I immediately got involved with as many church activities as I could. (More evidence for June that I'd truly lost my mind.) The choir director even approached me to sing in the choir and when I told him that I sounded like a frog he said, "We need male voices, and if you will just come to the choir practices, we will put you next to two good bass voices, and you can follow them."

I agreed and I fell in love with choir work and singing harmony.

I joined our adult Sunday School class and began studying the Bible. It was wonderful. One young deacon in particular, Charlie Rucker, impressed me with his knowledge and understanding. But I always felt like everyone in the class was a better Christian and much smarter about biblical principles.

I also began thinking seriously about my prayer life and the miracle of answered prayer. I knew without a doubt that God does answer prayer, but I had been a child the last time I'd earnestly gone to him with an urgent and specific request. Had it been too long? Would God listen? My wonderful wife was not a Christian; I wanted so much for her to find the happiness I had found. I determined that I would pray every day that Christ would be revealed to June and that she would receive him. Shortly thereafter, we began spending more time together. I began to travel much less than before, and when I did, June went with me. Our son was old enough, and my mother-in-law lived around the corner from us. Traveling with June was fun, but every once in a while I would catch her watching me like a hawk watches its victim. I hoped beyond hope it was because she was noticing my spiritual growth and wasn't plotting something sinister!

## About Miracles

The first miracle of answered prayer I could remember was shortly after my conversion experience. I had a little mutt dog named "Queenie". I was the only one in the world that loved her. And she loved me. Queenie disappeared one day and was gone for almost a month. I missed her so much. One morning I prayed to God that she was not dead, and would return home. I always talked to God, but this was a formal prayer. As I closed my prayer, I heard a whine, and in the doorway was Queenie. She was dirty and ragged and came leaping into my arms. I thanked the Lord that morning.

Another miracle happened a few years later. I had managed to get a paper route to help my mother and obtain some spending money. I collected weekly from my customers and paid my paper bill. One Friday I had finished collecting, and was riding my bicycle to the paper station to pay my bill, and I felt in my back pocket for my wallet and it was gone. I was heartsick. I parked my bicycle, put it on the kick stand and sat down on the curb and cried. I began to pray that God would help me find my wallet. I closed my prayer, lifted my eyes, and there before me was my wallet. It had caught in the forks of the luggage carrier that carried my paper bags. I thanked the Lord and rejoiced in the miracle.

Miracles have been defined as an occurrence that breaks the laws of nature. Many philosophers believe that since the laws of nature cannot be broken, there can be no miracles, only coincidences. To the believer, however, and especially to me, a miracle is a something that only God could have accomplished. I believe there are no coincidences! Pap-Paw

I was introduced to Biblical stewardship by a sermon I heard Dr. Hodge preach. I believed it with all my heart, but I also had many questions. I approached one of our deacons about the subject of giving 10% of your income to the church, and he explained it in simple terms. I understood that this part of your Christian life was personal—between you and God. I studied all the Scriptures that were given to me.

"Will a man rob God? Yet ye have robbed me. But ye say, Wherein have we robbed thee? In tithes and offerings. Ye are cursed with a curse; for ye have robbed me, even this whole nation. Bring ye all the tithes into the storehouse, that there may be meat in mine house, and prove me now herewith, saith the LORD of hosts, if I will not open you the windows of heaven, and pour you out a blessing, that there shall not be room enough to receive it." **Malachi 3:8-10**

"Woe to you, teachers of the law and Pharisees, you hypocrites! You give a tenth of your spices—mint, dill and cumin. But you have neglected the more important matters of the law—justice, mercy and faithfulness. You should have practiced the latter, without neglecting the former." **Matthew 23:23**

Since all of the related verses, especially Malachi, suggested putting God to the test, I decided to take Him up on the offer and begin tithing.

The first week I wrote a check. June looked at it and gasped, "Kessler, have you lost your mind? We can't even pay our bills right now." (We had begun calling ourselves Mr. and Mrs. Bill Debt). We clashed. I tried to explain how I felt about it—scared but confident in God at the same time—to no avail. Frustrated, I tore the check in half and walked out of the room. I continued to pray about it— after confessing my temper tantrum—and decided it was important enough to stick to my convictions. I told June I was going to do this as an act of obedience and not just to prove a point. She gave in, reluctantly, realizing that I had made up my mind and was proceeding in good conscience.

God is so true. From that moment in 1955 to the present, we have been faithful in the tithe and been able to give love offerings as well. We have also been able to pay our bills. Before that we were always late or unable to pay.

A few days later she asked, "You seem so happy and satisfied, is belonging to the church doing that for you?"

I told her it was not the church, but an intimate relationship with Jesus that gave me peace and a renewed sense of joy in my life. I confessed that I had accepted Jesus when I was a young boy but had never matured as a Christian. It was the first time I had ever tried to explain my past and my beliefs to her. I felt vulnerable and hurt when she retorted, "Boy, you must have lost it somewhere." But I persisted, and I think she started to better understand what had happened in my life. She finally agreed that she had seen the recent change.

"I wish something like that could happen to me."

"It can."

I began to share with her what I had learned from Scriptures about becoming a true Christian. About Romans 3:23, "For all have sinned and come short of the glory of God." She had no trouble believing that I was a sinner—and she admitted that she and all people were as well. I explained Romans 6:23, "The wages of sin is death, but the gift of God is eternal life through Jesus Christ our Lord".

"Kessler, do you think I could become a Christian and be as happy as you seem to be?"

This was it! This was the opportunity I had been praying for—O God, don't let me blow it. I then read her Romans 10:9-10, "That if thou shalt confess with thy mouth the Lord Jesus, and shalt believe in thine heart that God hath raised him from the dead, thou shalt be saved. For with the heart man believeth unto righteousness; and with the mouth confession is made unto salvation". I looked in her eyes and saw . . . well, I saw that she had heard me, but nothing else seemed to have happened.

"God, I trust you with June, please soften her heart."

One week from that day, we knelt in the front room by the fire and prayed together, and she very sweetly invited Jesus into her heart to be her Lord and Savior. Praise the Lord Almighty! Of course, it was the entire church family praying for her that made the difference; she was hard headed and stubborn and no amount of Scripture quoting was going to win her over. The very next Sunday, she and my son attended services. When the time came she went forward, followed by our son, and they professed their faith in Christ and were both baptized.

---

> The book of Romans is a wonderful book of the Bible and certainly gives a complete plan of salvation.

---

Not long after, I began teaching 10 year old boys in Sunday School. June joined the Women's Missionary Union, fondly referred to as the "WMU", and Ron was active in the Youth Department. Our family was, once again, a very happy unit. I was later ordained as a deacon in the church, and Dr. Hodge must have sensed that God was going to call me into the Gospel Ministry because he kept grooming me and sending me on mission preaching assignments. I preached at Rescue Missions, and various Lodge meetings, and other gatherings where a speaker was needed.

# There Will Be Hardship

**Back Story**

The first real trauma in my son's life came one night when he was visiting my mother in her home. One of my mother's lady friends was having an affair with a local fireman. The woman and her boyfriend came to her house. My mother wanted them to leave, but in walked the woman's husband with a hand gun and began to shoot the boyfriend. My mother and son were terrified because they were not sure if the husband would shoot them as well. The husband fired three shots into the boyfriend, and as he begged for his life, the husband shot him twice more. He then turned the gun on his wife, and my mother pleaded with him to spare her life. My little son just stood there too terrified to speak. The husband put the gun down and walked out.

Across the street from us lived a family with a young teenage boy—one of Ron's good friends in fact. His name was Bill. My wife and I both had seen evidence that his home life was difficult, and we were concerned but not surprised when he ran away to live with his grandmother. Three months later we received news that he had gotten a young girl pregnant. They had married and divorced before the baby was a year old.

Bill had since moved back with his parents, and it was very apparent that the same troubles existed. The young man did not seem to fit anywhere, and I fully intended to go and see if I could help him get on his feet; however, I was either too busy or too tired or had some other reason for not reaching out to him. I figured I'd get to it eventually—it wasn't an emergency type situation as far as I could see.

One afternoon, as June and I were pulling into the driveway, our son came running across the street crying to us that Bill had shot himself. Ron testified to the police that he had been talking on the phone when Bill came in with a revolver and a bullet stating that he intended to play "Russian Roulette". He placed the bullet in the cylinder, spun it, put the gun to his head and fired. It was that quick. My son thought, at first, that Bill was just faking, and the bullet was a blank, but as the blood began to spill on the floor, he knew his friend had just killed himself in front of him.

Investigators were unable to determine whether Bill was showing off or had deliberately committed suicide. We will never know, but either way, Bill's tragic death hit me hard. Here I was, a deacon in my church, living directly across from a lad that I knew was troubled, and I had done nothing. I was riddled with guilt and an overwhelming sense of responsibility for what had happened. God had led me to Bill, I had neglected to respond, and now the opportunity, and Bill, was gone. I was crushed with the knowledge that I had failed in my ministry. I prayed with a broken heart that God would forgive me, and I believe he did as he had done before, again and again. I promised God that if ever an opportunity to witness for Him, speak for Him, or defend His causes should arise, that I would act immediately and not put it off. 1 John 1:9 helped me get through this troubling time; it assured me of God's love and forgiveness:" If we confess our sins, He is faithful and just to forgive us of our sins and cleanse us from all unrighteousness."

Now, I have been a preacher and pastor for almost 50 years, and I will share my calling in a later chapter. I just want the reader to know that I do not intend to do a lot of preaching in this book, but I do want to establish that I accept the Bible as God's Word, without error, and the best thing I have found to guide me. Kessler

**Love Sick**

Ron was absolutely crazy about a girl named Peggy who lived in our neighborhood. I loved to tease him about it. One afternoon while we were watching television, he began talking about Peggy. I said, "Son, let me demonstrate how you act about Peggy." I then pretended Peggy was coming down the street, and, pretending to be my son. I crawled to the door saying, "Peggy . . . Peggy, oh please Peggy." My son said, "Aw Daddy," and we both doubled over with laughter. Still do to this day!

When my son was sixteen, he met a girl named Martha Archer. Her parents had divorced, and she now lived with her father and stepmother. I adored Martha and gave her a big hug every time she came to visit. Martha told me on one occasion that no one in her family had ever hugged her or told her that they loved her. My heart ached for her, and I hugged her that much more tightly from then on. I did not realize how serious Ron and Martha were about each other. I guess I was too busy with other things to notice.

Martha made a trip to Odessa, Texas, to see her mother, and she and my son corresponded back and forth. June opened and read one of the letters. I know she should not have done this, but she did. She came into the room looking pale with the letter still in her hand.

"Kessler, Martha is pregnant."

I felt like I'd just had all the air knocked out of me. They were so young.

I accompanied Mr. Archer to Odessa to pick up his daughter. I wanted Martha to know that I loved her and would stand behind her. Thankfully, abortion was never mentioned, nor considered. We were assured that they were very much in love and wanted to be with each other the rest of their lives. Mr. Archer wanted the two of them to get married right away; we all wanted both of them to finish school.

I suggested that we receive counsel from Dr. Hodge, my pastor. On that much, we all agreed. Dr. Hodge listened to everything everyone had to say, offered some sound advice, and most importantly, prayed with us and for us.

Martha and Ronald Kessler were married, left school before finishing, moved into our house, and on January 7, 1960, Glenda Renee' Kessler was born. She was named Glenda after June's deceased sister, and Renee' after June's mother. The night the baby was brought home was a complete disaster. No one knew what to do. The next day, I asked one of the church nursery workers, Joy, to come and help us. What a blessing—and life saver—she was! She knew exactly what to do, and ended up staying with us a full week.

## Pride and Joy

I was a proud grandfather and was rather pleased that I had reached grandfather status at age thirty-six. June was an equally proud grandmother who was perfectly content to have the entire family living under the same roof. As far as we were concerned, our granddaughter was pure and could do no wrong. And then, my bubble burst. I had picked Glenda up with both hands, holding her under the arms, and extended my arms so that I could gaze on her with delight. She wiggled and giggled, and then slammed both hands against my ears. Thought my brain had exploded. I put her down very fast and decided that she was not as sinless as I imagined.

June also experienced Glenda's feisty side. She had the teeth prints on her arm to prove it, but she loved the child all the more for it. One day, the toddler got into the cabinet and spilled an entire bottle of olives on the floor. June and Ron came running in when they heard the crash, and when it was apparent that Glenda was unhurt,

June said something to the effect that accidents will happen, and began to clean up the mess.

My son was incredulous. "Is that woman my mother?" "That's not the mother I remember. Had I done that she would have paddled me good!"

I advised him that one day, if he were very lucky, he would understand.

## Change is Constant

My sales manager, George Feus, was in town wanting a conference with me. I did not think much about it because he came at least once per year. As was his custom, he took June and me out to a nice restaurant for dinner.

June very jokingly said, "George, sometimes I wish I were thousands of miles from here."

George replied, "It is strange that you would say that because I came here to offer your husband a job in California."

June stammered, "I was only kidding."

I was advised that J.K. Smit & Sons had bought out a diamond tool company in Los Angeles, California, and needed a sales representative there. All the company salesmen had been considered, and I was the one chosen. I asked for time to pray about it, and I was given three days to make my decision. June and I prayed together about the offer. Although it meant leaving our families, we both seemed to know that it was God's plan for us. We then talked it over with Ron and Martha; they were both very happy for us about the job, but not about us moving to California. Ron had secured employment at Houston Light & Power Company as a meter reader, and we all decided it was best for them to stay and continue to live in our house. I flew to Los Angeles, met the personnel there, rented an apartment nearby, and returned to Houston. We loaded up a U-Haul trailer and drove to Los Angeles. June cried the entire trip and nothing I did seemed to help.

About half way through the very long trip, I quipped, "If you will just shut up crying, I promise that I will move them to California!"

She was so relieved that, thankfully for me, she either didn't hear or simply decided to disregard my harshness.

It didn't take long, and we were ready for them to come. June and I met them at the train station, and I shall never forget the reunion there. Glenda and June spotted each other from about two hundred yards away and began running toward one another with Glenda screaming, "Mam-Maw, Mam-Maw!"

We had found a home to live in, and now it was time to go in search of a church home for us. I noticed that the Southern Baptist churches were much smaller than the other denominations. I later found out that Southern Baptists had waited a long time to move into California. I was used to larger churches, but was impressed with First Southern Baptist of Hawthorne and the pastor, Charles Perdue. June and I moved our membership, and then Ron moved his. Martha was converted to Christ and was baptized there.

The small church was growing. We were all involved in various church activities, and I was asked to serve as a deacon since I was already ordained and had served in Texas. I took charge of the sports program and became coach of the basketball team. My son was one of our best players. All the teams in the church league were much better than us; however, we were successful at reaching young couples through the program, and we eventually began to win our fair share of games.

Everything was good. Ron had obtained employment at Edison Company, the local electricity producer, as a meter reader. He liked his job, and it appeared he would have advancement opportunities very quickly. Martha made an announcement that she was with child again, and on December 8, 1963, Tracy Ann Kessler was born. I guess Ron and Martha took seriously the Biblical encouragement to "be fruitful and multiply". Tracy was not named after any family members. Martha liked the name very much, and I was so in love with the child, I didn't care at that time. Strange, but when your child is named, it seems odd at first; however, in no time the name fits perfectly.

---

**Martha . . .**

. . . was born to bear children. She told me many times that she had experienced stomach aches that were worse than the pains of having a baby. When she was ready to deliver this time, she tried in vain to convince the hospital nurses that they should get her to the delivery room and quick, but the nurses would not take her seriously. Tracy was born on the way to the delivery room. I was standing in the hallway and could see my grandchild lying on her mother's stomach. I know that all grandparents think that their grandbabies are the most beautiful ever born, but in all seriousness, mine *really were* beautiful. God had blessed us with two healthy, gorgeous little girls. (There were more to come!)

---

Tracy was a delight; she seemed to appreciate everything so much. I took both girls to the store when Tracy was a toddler and told them to pick out what they wanted. Glenda was rapidly selecting from every bin, and Tracy was slowly looking over all the options. Finally, she reached down and picked up one single piece of bubble gum.

I said, "Baby, is that all you want?"

She replied, "This is what I want."

I added some more things to her selection.

Both girls also loved to visit us at our home. June kept the pantry well stocked with "goodies", and I do not recall a single time that they left without a "goodie bag" from Mam-Maw.

It was during this decade that the Korean War ended and the Vietnam War began. I never fully understood either conflict: why they couldn't be avoided, why there were so many limitations put on the military, or why politics and the division along party lines played such a role. As technology exploded, the moral fiber of America seemed to implode. Church attendance began to decline: more and more people lost interest or just got too busy with other things.

Young people started what was coined the "hippie movement". The movement originally started in San Francisco, California, when a large number of hippies gathered at the corner of Haight Street and Ashbury Street, which came to be known as the Haight-Ashbury District. Hippies created their own communities, listened to psychedelic rock, embraced the sexual revolution, and some used drugs. They said they were out to promote the message of peace, but many of them used the movement as an excuse to rebel against more than America's involvement in the Vietnam War. They rebelled against everything, everyone, and every establishment.

Vietnam was not a popular war by any means. The American people witnessed the conflict from our living rooms. We watched as reporters interviewed disgruntled soldiers complaining that the rules of engagement set up by our government were handicapping them in combat. Casualty tallies popped up on the television screen every evening and the numbers were horrible. Our wounded men started coming home with lost arms and legs and massive head injuries. Civilians and soldiers alike were caught up in the many divisive issues troubling America at the time; the validity of the war: civil rights, the role of government and the irrelevance of the Church.

# 1963-1973

## Do Your Homework

At a morning service in the early 60's, I announced to the church that God was calling me into the pastoral ministry. The congregants did not seem surprised at all; however, June was shocked. In hindsight, it would have been kinder to June had I told her *before* I broadcasted my revelation. She anxiously revealed her doubts.

"Kessler, I don't feel Him calling me."

"Honey, He is not calling you, He is calling me. Your calling is to follow me."

I realize this is hard for most wives to understand, and many who have found themselves in that position have chosen to leave their husbands because of it, but June was different. I assured her that God was not calling me to quit my job and that the next step was for me to enroll in seminary extension courses. Things moved a little quicker than I had first imagined, though, and the church ordained me to the Gospel Ministry in 1964. On Pastor Perdue's recommendation, I was given the title of Associate Pastor.

> The ordination service was beautiful, and very inspirational. I was given a Thompson Chain Reference Bible as a gift from the church. The Bible has been rebound and rebound. I retired it many years ago and it is now in Ron's possession.

A couple in our church expressed their intention to marry—the man had been married and divorced; the woman had never been married. Brother Perdue had strong convictions that no one should remarry if they were divorced, so he came to me and asked if I would be willing to perform the ceremony. Was it a trick question? I answered quickly. "If it is wrong for you to do it, why would it be right for me to do it?"

It would have been better for me to ask God before I answered. The couple left the church, joined another, and had no problem at all getting married.

Obviously, ministers hold various views on this subject, and at the time, I was not sure what to think. One of the pastors had to be wrong, right? I made myself a pledge that if I ever got to seminary I was going to research the subject and decide for myself.

Some years later, I wrote a term paper on the subject using research from both the Old and New Testaments. What follows is a condensed version of my conclusion:

**The Christian cannot look to the Old Testament text as a guide for marital problems.** The Mosaic Law allows for divorce should the husband find "some unseemly thing" in the wife (Deuteronomy. 24:1-4). Is that "unseemly thing" finding the wife to be unfaithful, or was it that she burned the toast or lost her looks?

**Each case should be looked at individually, with the approach being the ultimate spiritual welfare of the individual.** The teachings of Jesus leave no Scriptural grounds for divorce unless the "except for" clause is accepted (Matthew 19:7-9), which still leaves no place for remarriage. While there are no Scriptural grounds for divorce and remarriage, the teachings of Christ are principles of ideal nature and not laws, and apply only to Christian couples. It is entirely possible for sin to completely destroy the ideal and so pervert the marriage on the part of one or both spouses, that sometimes divorce may be the lesser of the two evils. It is feasible to believe that Jesus can forgive sins dealing with marriage and divorce, just as with any other sin in the Christian's life.

**A person's belief status makes a difference.** Paul teaches that in the case of mixed marriages—where one spouse is a believer and the other is not—should the unbeliever wish to stay, the believer should let them stay in hope of converting them. I believe that the clause "unless some ungodly demand is placed upon them" is inherent. Should the unbeliever leave, the believer is no longer under the marriage bond; the believer is free of the bond and is free to remarry.

I received an 'A' on my research paper with a note from the professor that commended me for taking a very compassionate approach to divorce and remarriage.

Although he was loved by a majority of the young couples, there were some who wanted to get rid of Pastor Purdue. This troublesome group held secret meetings, plotted ways to vacate the pulpit, walked out as soon as he stood up to preach, and more than once threw garbage on the pastor's lawn. The disrespect shown to Pastor Perdue hit an all-time low when a choir member/Deacon came forward to sing a solo, and instead proceeded to announce that he was calling a meeting to vacate the pulpit and install the music director as pastor. (The music director was well aware of the deacon's plan.) The plot failed because the constitution and bi-laws of the church stated that only the pastor could moderate a business meeting unless he appointed someone else. An authentic meeting was called shortly after the last incident, and the involved members and their families were voted out of the church. In spite of my efforts at restoration, irreparable damage had been done; the church was split, and was never the same again. Had I known before what Brother Perdue confessed to me later—that he had been trying to leave for over a year, but because all he had to his name were his clothes and his worn out Ford Falcon—I might have been able to prevent some of the fallout.

I learned some things from this church problem that helped me in my future pastorates. Differences of opinion are healthy in a church, like in a family, if they are handled in a mature, respectful manner. It is best to address these differences early rather than waiting for them to become divisive. It is an insult to the integrity of the Church when the members squabble like spoiled brats. Praise the Lord that very few churches go through this. In the three churches I was to pastor in the future, there would never be any divisions.

The pastor left and the young couples I had worked so hard to reach and develop felt betrayed. I am sad to say that, one by one, four precious families became discouraged and left the church, and to my knowledge, never joined another. My own son and daughter-in-law were so hurt and angry that they stopped regular attendance, although they did allow June and me to take the girls to church and Sunday School with us each week. Someday, those who caused this split will have to give an answer for their actions.

I agreed to serve as Interim Pastor at the church until a suitable replacement could be found. As soon as possible, a "Pulpit Committee" was formed, trained, and charged to begin the search. The process took a while, as I had fully anticipated, but even after the system was in place, I saw little evidence that the committee was adamant about finding someone. When I mentioned my concerns, I was told that the members were happy with me and they did not want to consider anyone else for the position. I told them I planned to attend seminary for pastoral training whenever the opportunity came, but that in the meantime, I was busy enough with all my current pastoral duties. I encouraged them to prayerfully and diligently find our next pastor.

## The Pitch

We may have been pastorless, but our sports outreach program was thriving! We now had a softball team as well as a basketball team. I did not coach the softball team, nor did I play on it; I was too old to compete with the young men. Hard to admit, but then, the point was to reach young couples through the love of the game, and that I did. As an added bonus, we fielded a great softball team. The league was very competitive, and First Southern Baptist of Gardena had won the tournament trophy several years in a row. Although our team was better, they had an AAA pitcher that was almost untouchable. We had a weak link . . . pitching. Our problem? We walked too many batters. I had been pitching batting practice for our team, and although I wasn't good, I was able to throw strikes across the plate. At one of the games, one of our young men suggested that I pitch the games, and let the opposition hit. The reasoning was that since we had such a strong fielding team, we were better off letting the opponent put the ball in the air. We tried it, I had a great time pitching, and we beat Gardena that year. The trophies were awarded in our church on a Sunday night. Much to my surprise, I was voted most valuable player by my teammates and awarded a beautiful trophy. I treasured that trophy more than any I had ever won because it came from my son and a very special group of wonderful young men.

## Pap-Paw's Pride

One of our favorite family outings was to drive up to Mount Baldy and play in the snow. Southern California is unique. It is entirely possible to visit the sandy beaches and the snowy mountains all in one day. The beach and Mount Baldy are only hours apart. On one occasion at Mount Baldy, the snow had been rather heavy, and Glenda and Tracy were busy making a snow man. Ron picked up Terri and was carrying her through the snow. Hold on! Have I not told you about the birth of my third granddaughter? Terri Lynn Kessler was born on July 21, 1966, just as beautiful as her two older sisters. Back to the story—Terri looked at her dad and said, "Daddy, I don't like the snow, let's go to the movies."

June quickly tired of the cold, as well, and wanted to leave before the rest of the family lost their enthusiasm. On the way home, we stopped several time so the girls could feed what they'd saved of their lunches to the critters at a roadside stop. They would bend down and call, "Here little quirls, here little birdies." To say my heart was full would be an understatement.

# The Right Word Makes a Difference

Jack and Louella White were dear friends that June and I began socializing with after they had come to me for counseling. When Jack suddenly died of a heart attack, not only were we put to the test, but so was God. Louella was understandably devastated. June and I joined her at the Catholic hospital where one of the nuns came up to Louella and said, "Mrs. White, it was just God's will."

Louella was furious and railed at the poor nun. I tried in vain to offer wise advice and comforting words, but I was not making much headway. June was doing a much better job consoling Louella than I was. I even tried to explain some Biblical truths, but she said, "Les, when Jack had the attack and they took him in the ambulance, I prayed that God would allow me to speak to my husband before he died, and He let me down."

Although a devout Christian, Louella was angry at God. I tried to explain God's perfect timetable, His sovereignty, and His ability to use all things for good in those who love Him. I knew her emotions wouldn't allow her to understand, but I desperately wanted to help her find peace in that horrible situation. When I spoke next, I think the words I used were, "Louella, Jack could have already been dead by the time you prayed that prayer."

It may have helped some, but the resultant tears told me not much. Again, June was the real comfort to our dear friend; she listened without offering advice, cried with her without apology, and eventually laughed with her as they shared memories of more pleasant times. Louella would go on to make a great life for herself, and the three of us remained close friends for many years. Because her three daughters: Debbie, Becky and Glenna became extremely active in Louella's life, we were fortunate enough to call them friends as well.

# **Unconditional**

Ron and Martha were under a lot of financial pressure, so Ron made the decision to take a part-time job at a drive-in movie theater. He requested to work on Friday and Saturday nights; time that he would typically spend with his wife and three daughters. I was not in favor of it. It took valuable time away from his family, made Sundays the only day he could recover from the week, and put strain on Martha as she would now have very little support caring for the girls. I feared it would interfere with his spiritual life; decisions that seem simple and of little consequence can become the jumping off place for much more critical choices. Ron assured me that he would be able to attend church on Sunday nights, but I felt in my heart that it would not work that way.

Several weeks later, I learned from a friend that my son was having an affair with a co-worker at the drive-in. Ron and I were together in his car when I confronted him about his relationship with the woman. It is true that there are always two sides to every family problem, but regardless of the circumstances at home, I knew Ron's actions would lead to heartache and misery. I warned him of the very real possibility that he could lose his family and everything he held dear. He listened respectfully, but he didn't acknowledge what I was saying. Hoping that my own experience with infidelity would soften his heart, I shared my past problems and the consequences of my behavior. I assured him that God could heal all wounds and encouraged him not to give up on his marriage. I even quoted his grandfather's words of wisdom after he had divorced my mother. "Son, don't ever leave your first love. I did and have been miserable ever since."

My advice was well received, but he did not take it. When he asked me, "Dad, do you still love me?" I confirmed what I preach. True love does not end when things go wrong. True love says, "I love you, and there is nothing you could possibly do that would destroy that love." I knew the coming days would be extremely difficult for both Martha and Ron.

## Are You Ready for Some Miracles?

I was on a sales trip to the northern bay area and called on a semiconductor plant in Sunnyvale, California—Tempress Industries. I had called on the president several times for the purpose of selling him our diamond wheels for grinding diamond scribing tools. Mr. Christensen seemed to like me very much, but advised me that he had a yearly contract with one of my competitors and wasn't moving his business at this time. However, he was in the market for someone new to mount his diamonds and wondered if my company was interested at the price of $1.25 each in quantities of 2000. He gave me a small sample of diamonds, and I sent them to my home office with the request for a quote.

My employer called me the next week. "Les, we don't want anything to do with it. We are returning the diamonds to you."

On the trip back to Tempress to return the diamonds to Mr. Christensen, I said to myself, "I believe I could set those diamonds in my garage." As soon as I arrived, I sat down with Mr. Christiansen, explained my calling to the pastoral ministry, and expressed my desire to attend seminary. I'm sure he was a little confused at exactly why I was sharing my personal goals with him. But when I told him that the company I worked for was not equipped to set his diamonds, and that I would like to try it myself and use the extra income to pay for schooling, he immediately embraced the idea. He gave me a packet of loose diamonds to take home and experiment with and offered to help in any way necessary.

Setting the diamonds turned out to be much harder than I thought. I knew I could figure it out; I just needed to be creative. I put together some very crude fixtures using a used vacuum cleaner and an old metalworking lathe and made several unsuccessful attempts. But with every failure, I learned something new and important. Most of my ideas came in the wee hours of the morning as I was lying in bed thinking about the process. Many times I would get up and go out to the garage in the middle of the night to see if what I was thinking would work. Things didn't often develop as I had seen them in my mind's eye, but I was making progress. Eventually, I figured it out and my process became both efficient and effective.

It wasn't long before I felt that I was ready to inform my employer, J. K. Smit and Sons that I would be leaving to enter seminary. They were not surprised at all. They congratulated me, flew me to Murray Hill, New Jersey, for a farewell dinner, and treated me to a New York Giants baseball game.

The next step was to enroll in Golden Gate Baptist Theological Seminary in Mill Valley, California, and find suitable housing. The campus was beautiful, located just across the Golden Gate Bridge, and it took no time at all to finish my business there. I had no idea how hard it would be to find a place to live. I required at least two bedrooms and a garage large enough to set up my diamond setting equipment. I had only one day, so I checked with a local real estate agent. The agent almost laughed.

"What you are seeking is impossible to find in this area. We only have one listing in a five mile radius of Mill Valley."

The house was perfect: a two bedroom, two bath, with a garage and a basement with all the wiring I needed already in place. The rent was $330 per month, which was very cheap given the affluence of the neighborhood. Today, this same place would rent for at least $2000 per month, maybe more.

## I Know the Plans I Have For You

I returned home to find that my son and daughter-in-law had separated. Our hearts were grieved because we loved them all so much. June was very worried.

"Kessler, what are we going to do? You have resigned your job, we are supposed to move, and the kids (our name for Martha and Ron) are separated."

I honestly had no answers except to turn it all over to God. God's answer was a little voice within my soul that simply said, "Get up and go, and I will go with you."

I want to emphasize how close and personal the Heavenly Father can be to His children. A peace and calm came over my soul, and at over 40 years of age, I bid my church family at First Southern Baptist of Hawthorne a warm goodbye. My son helped me load up a U-Haul truck and trailer with all our belongings. June and I were in the truck, Ron drove my old Buick, and we began our move to San Anselmo, California.

The move was quite an experience. On the way, we encountered the worst rainstorm Northern California had experienced in 50 years. My son helped unload, and to this day he testifies how heavy boxes of books feel, especially carrying them upstairs.

I enrolled at seminary the next day and was informed that my Associate in Science degree from University of Houston was not acceptable; however, because I was over forty, they would accept me as a "diploma student". All the courses would be the same, with the exception that I would not be allowed to take the Hebrew and Greek classes for credit, but could monitor them. I would be taking the full three-year program and would graduate with a "Diploma in Theology" instead of the "Master of Divinity" degree. The other option would have been to go back to college and obtain a Bachelor of Arts degree. I felt that the important thing was the education, not the degree, so I opted for the diploma and have never been sorry.

In the year 1967, Ron was fired. It seemed apparent that his compulsive drinking and drug usage had a lot to do with his inability to keep his job at Edison Company. This put Martha and the children in an even more precarious position than they were already in. June and I loved Martha like our own child. We shared our lives with her and the girls with authenticity and genuine affection even as our relationship with our son became strained. Just like my parents and in-laws had done for June and Ron when I was serving abroad, I felt a great responsibility for seeing to the financial needs of Martha and the children. I located a small apartment in Fairfax, California— adjacent to San Anselmo—and I gave Martha my Buick. We shared meals, bought the girls clothing, and helped in any way we could. I have to admit that I felt overwhelmed at the task of carrying a full academic load at seminary, running my business, and now looking out for my extended family, but it was the right thing to do, and I knew it.

I registered my business as "Trinity Company". I chose that name because I knew that my Father, my Jesus, and the precious Holy Spirit had put the whole thing together. I would make $1.25 per tool, and at 3000 tools per month, it was more money than I had ever made in my life.

I never forgot hearing God say, "Get up and go, and I will go with you." I realized that I would not have been able to accomplish this on my own.

I said to my Heavenly Father in prayer, "Dear Lord, if you will take care of my business, I will try to the best of my ability to take care of yours." I entered into a partnership with God that day, and it has been an exciting adventure ever since.

I had already started Martha setting diamonds, and hired two seminary students' wives to help as well. I also included Glenda and Tracy in manufacturing. Glenda was seven, Tracy was four, and Terri was one. Glenda and Tracy loved it and were good at cleaning out the metal shanks and getting them ready on a "setting board". Terri's "job" was to accompany me to seminary where she would be placed in the seminary daycare. The program was excellent, and she loved it. I was thrilled to be able to have lunch with her every day at the cafeteria; her favorite meal was a grilled cheese sandwich and root beer from the vending machine. I always gave Terri a quarter to get her root beer, and the machine would return fifteen cents. One day I gave her the exact change to put in the machine. It took a lot of effort to convince her that the machine had not stolen her nickel and dime.

Golden Gate had many missionary students; Terri fell in love with one such student named Lucy who would later be appointed by our Foreign Mission Board to Africa. Every time Terri and I would enter the cafeteria, she would see Lucy and shout, "There is Woocy!" and run to her table. Terri learned so much in the day care, and Martha's was so grateful that her daughter was well taken care of. Without the seminary facility, Martha would not have been able to afford early schooling for her youngest daughter. Through all of the trials of this stressful time, the six of us became very close as a family. June and I, however, did not get to see Ron as often as we would have liked. We worried about him, but he was a grown man and responsible for his own choices. There comes a time when you have to turn even your children over to God. I hoped for reconciliation for him and Martha, but it was just not to be.

## Knowledge that Surpasses Understanding

My first semester at seminary was very hectic; it had been twenty years since I had attended college, and I was not prepared for the academic requirements. The reading assignments alone were killing me. Speed Reading courses are well worth it! It seemed as though each professor thought his class was the only one on anyone's schedule. All the students, not just me, complained about the homework being assigned. I struggled especially hard with theological terms until someone directed me to a book entitled "Handbook of Theological Terms". What a blessing! Thankfully, though, I got along well with almost all my professors—I was about the same age as the majority of them—and they seemed to like me as well. I even received golf invitations on occasion even though my heavy schedule prevented me from participating most of the time.

June and I visited several churches in the area and finally selected First Southern Baptist Church of San Anselmo. We joined by transfer of letter (membership), and I discovered that most of my professors belonged to that church. One Sunday I was invited to preach the morning service. I got up to speak and looked out over the congregation, and there they all were. I was scared, but I reminded myself that every one of those men wanted me to succeed in and out of the classroom. This realization gave me courage, and my opening remarks were something like this, "I am so grateful for the opportunity to skin a bunch of professors." They roared in laughter, and after the service I was clapped on the back and extended many enthusiastic handshakes. Then I was informed that they would see me the next day on campus.

I had one lady professor who taught a class on ministering to children. As a grandfather, this class that emphasized children's sermons, held a place in my heart that the younger students couldn't imagine. I had always done children's sermons at First Southern Hawthorne, but this class helped me understand the importance of stories. I have been a joyful storyteller ever since!

After one month on campus, I felt that something was missing. I had a pastor's heart, and one morning on the way to campus I was deep in conversation with God. "Father, you know the plans you have for me. You know what is best. If you think I can handle it, and if it is your will for me, I would love the opportunity to be a pastor of a small church. Please open that door for me and make it clear that I should step through it!"

On my lunch hour that very same day, the Director of Missions in Calaveras County came to my table and introduced himself. He said that one of my professors had given him my name and asked me if I would be willing to preach at a Baptist church in West Point, California—150 miles away—the coming Sunday; the church was looking for a pastor. I had shared with June my prayer on the way to Seminary for God to open the door to some small church. I had no idea it would be a 300 mile round trip, but I was sure this was the answer I was looking for.

June and I arrived the following Sunday, and by that evening I was called to be the church's new pastor. After praying with June for God's guidance and discernment, I promised to give them an answer by the following Sunday. The following Sunday I accepted the call as pastor of First Baptist Church of West Point, California. I was not sure how I was going to pastor the church, continue the full academic load at seminary, and ship 3000 tools per month to Tempress Industries. I had already decided that if I was going to finish the three year program, it would require taking classes year-round, so there would be no summer break to catch my breath. I would have to rely on my employees to get the physical work done. I would have to learn to budget my time well. I would have to be consciously aware that every moment was precious and make fostering my relationships with June, Martha and the children a priority. The girls were such a joy and were always ready to be with Pap-Paw and Mam-Maw. I look back and say to myself, "It was humanly impossible," but of course, with God all things are possible.

---

The town of West Point, California, had a population of 500 and was founded by Kit Carson as he pioneered through California. There was an animal trough just outside of town that was fed water by an underground spring. The historical spot was famous because, as the pioneers passed through, they would water their stock there. The spring is famous for its cool, delicious water. Visitors to the area would fill up their containers with the refreshing spring water. West Point was located just off Highway 88 in the foothills of the Sierra Mountains, approximately 3000 feet above sea level. The scenery was so beautiful it would almost take your breath away.

---

June and I would leave our house in San Anselmo on Friday afternoons after seminary classes were over and head for our church in West Point. My Buick got approximately 12 miles to a gallon of gas. Gasoline was thirty-eight cents a gallon in those days. I would spend Saturday studying for sermons and do my entire visitation. A deacon named Illus Ball and his wife Mary, who had helped start the church twenty years earlier, let us stay in a small garage apartment next to their home. Brother Ball was a retired lumberjack and had a thriving little business on the side sharpening chain saws for the local lumbermen and repairing small engines. Mary Ball was a great cook, and on Sunday evenings after the service, she routinely invited June and me for a "little dab" of something to eat. One of her specialties was canned peaches. She harvested her own fruit and put them up in quart jars.

I never left hungry, but the trip home was painful. I would be so fatigued and sleepy that June would have to keep me awake by talking to me about anything that came to mind. I depended on highway speed bumps to alert me when I had dozed off and crossed the center line. Travel made the pastorate in West Point hard for me, but at no time did I ever feel that I should give it up. I felt at peace with my calling and my place of service. I was very fond of the people, and they all loved June.

## The Encounter

Our church family consisted of retirees, woodsmen who worked in the timber industry, and some families that liked living in the mountains and driving up to cabins on the weekends. I loved to go visiting and was always treated respectfully except on one occasion. Southern Baptists of California were working with Baptists of Texas in a joint venture named "Encounter California Crusade". The states exchanged pastors to preach for one another. I was not able to go to Texas; however, a Texas pastor was sent to me to hold services.

The Texas pastor was the epitome of the term "narrow minded". He was a good speaker with sound theology, but I was not comfortable with some of his personal views. For example, we were all sitting around Brother Ball's dining table one evening after service, and the subject of wayward adult children was raised. It seems this pastor's oldest son, upon reaching the age of nineteen, decided he did not want to go to church anymore. The Texas pastor said this to us about his son, "I just told him that if he made that decision, I would no longer be his father, and he would not be welcome at our house."

The preacher seemed very proud of his stand. I could not sit there in silence. The Balls looked at June, and June looked at me as if to say, "Well Kessler, say something!"

I knew our beloved son Ron had strayed, and two of the Ball's grown children had also stopped going to church, so I simply replied, "I only have one son, and there is nothing he could ever do that would make me deny him, or not rejoice to have him in my home at every opportunity possible." I followed with my testimony and enough details about my previous lifestyle to make his son look like a choir boy. The Texas preacher did not seem to take offense, but probably wrote me off as a liberal theologian.

The next day the Texas pastor and I went into the community visiting. We had some cordial receptions and one not so cordial. We knocked on this one door, and an elderly gentleman answered. I introduced myself and the Texas preacher, and advised him we were inviting people to hear the Texan preach. The man at the door said to me, "Reverend, I don't want to hurt your feelings and I believe in God, but as far as this Jesus Christ, he was nothing but a bastard child because there could be no way he could be born to a virgin." The Texan almost fell of the porch in shock, and I knew I had to reply. I prayerfully chose my words.

"Well sir, Jesus was either who He said He was, the Son of God, who came to earth as God Incarnate, or God in human flesh, or He was as you said, a child without an earthly father. I believe Him to be who He said He was in the Bible, and the only proof I have is my changed life and the changed, redeemed lives of millions of others."

I asked the man to pray about which truth was correct, and we left. My Texas consignment was silent on the way back to the church. Of all the wonderful preachers in Texas, I had to have one like this, but I learned anew and afresh the wonderful grace and forgiveness of the Heavenly Father as he works in the lives of individuals.

## A Breath of Fresh Air

The weather was cold, and the only heat I had in my basement workshop was a gas heater. I understood the importance of proper ventilation, so I was careful to keep the window and the door that led to the garage open at all times. One evening, June was upstairs by herself, and I was working downstairs in the shop. Our little poodle Suzette was with me. As I was standing at the lathe working, I felt a sudden, terrible throbbing in my head followed by nausea. I was sure it would pass, but the pain continued to worsen. Was I was catching the flu or something? I decided to lie down on an army cot I kept in the basement to rest for a minute. Things did not improve, and I decided to go upstairs to tell June. I could not get up. My mind was clear, but my body was not responding, my legs were paralyzed.

| Carbon monoxide poisoning is a silent killer. |

June heard what sounded like groaning and realized that the usual work noises were no longer coming from the basement. She rushed down the flight of stairs to check on me and found me pale and lifeless. She immediately called 911 and advised the operator that I was either having a heart attack or stroke or might possibly be dead. The emergency crew arrived within five minutes, and the next thing I knew there was a man with a big round face looking down at me from only inches away and asking, "Mr. Kessler, can you hear me? If you can hear me, blink your eyes." I had an oxygen mask on my face, but I blinked.

In what seemed like the far distance, I heard another fireman say, "I found the source of the carbon monoxide poisoning; it's this heater!" The rescue team also found that there had been no ventilation to the basement. Even in my confused state, I knew I always kept the window and the door open. I struggled to figure out what had happened. A breeze might have been able to shut the door a little bit, but not the window. The window takes an effort to shut, so I would have remembered doing that. To this day, no one has been able to explain the near catastrophe.

Although the oxygen seemed to be slowly clearing my thoughts, I still could not move my legs. The rescue worker that was standing over me told June that it appeared that the threat of death had passed, but that I was going to be taken to the hospital to make sure I didn't have brain damage. I assured June I was going to be alright, and then with alarm I remembered Suzette. June found our scared little dog cowering underneath the cot where there had been enough good air for her to survive.

I was taken to the hospital, examined, and released. The doctor was amazed. "You are a lucky man. One more minute, and you would have been dead. By all accounts you should also have suffered brain damage, but we cannot find evidence to suggest any long-term side effects."

> My wife was not good at handling little things, but in emergencies, she was always a very calm individual. In this case, she did all the right things to save my life. The unbeliever reading this book might say, "That was a coincidence." But to June and me, it was a miracle. I was beginning to appreciate that the longer a person lives, the more opportunities there are to look in retrospect at the past, and that is when you can see the hand of God most clearly.

June and I realized once again that God had more for me to do, and we were drawn closer to Him. This incident also strengthened our relationship with Martha and the children. The girls were so relieved that their Pap-Paw was going to be alright that I could hardly keep them out of my lap. Someone got word to Ron, and he rushed to San Anselmo to be with me. June and I were so glad to have him with us, and Martha and the children were ecstatic. The togetherness was a true blessing and worth every minute of the scare that brought us all together.

The time we enjoyed gave me hope that Martha and Ron would reconcile—I honestly felt they still loved each other. However, it never came to pass, and Ron left to go back to Southern California where he was involved in another relationship. I found out later that a child had been conceived, and it would be several more years before I would meet Ronda Kessler, born October 30, 1968.

## Team Work

One summer in West Point, I decided I would like to host a Vacation Bible School that would begin on a Monday and end the following Friday. I wouldn't be able to be the lead, but June was willing to stay on the church field in the garage apartment next to the Ball's residence to oversee things, and I planned to contact the Home Mission Board to see if I could get some assistance. I would be able to help wrap things up when I arrived on Friday after Seminary classes.

June and I approached the church with our plans fully expecting everyone to be excited, but no one seemed to want to participate. Apparently, VBS had been attempted before with dismal results. Very few of the residents of West Point wanted to send their children. June and I were surprised but undaunted; we organized the event and picked a date. It was agreed that a freshman missionary student named Cynthia Clawson would be sent to run the program for us. Cynthia had volunteered with youth groups during summer camps and had a passion for working with kids of all ages. She was also very skilled on the piano and possessed a beautiful singing voice. She was able to stay calm under pressure and handled emergencies with great skill; qualities that endeared her to almost everyone.

Of the seventy-five kids attending, there was one youth who was very disruptive and constantly disturbed the class. His name was Ralph, and he was a deacon's son and an active church member. Cynthia handled him beautifully.

"Ralph, are you a Christian?"

Ralph replied indignantly, "Of course I am. I belong to this church, I have been baptized, and my father is a deacon here."

Cynthia looked him square in the eyes and said, "Then, act like one."

This took the edge off of Ralph for a day or two, but he soon revamped his efforts to distract the other kids in the class. Cynthia was undaunted.

"Ralph, if you insist on this behavior, you are welcome to leave my class."

He quickly—and noisily—gathered his belongings and walked out allowing the door to bang shut behind him. But Ralph encountered something he wasn't expecting when he arrived home. His dad got him straight and sent him straight back to class with a well-practiced apology. The atmosphere in the classroom was much improved after that, and he and Cynthia got along fine.

> I followed Cynthia's career as she became a well-known and successful gospel recording artist. In later years, I saw her on stage a few times as she performed with the Bill Gaither Homecoming Group.

## Peer Pressure

Albert and his wife Audrey lived in Sacramento, but drove up to West Point on weekends. They would attend morning services at our church on Sunday and then drive home Sunday night. Albert had purchased a piece of property about fifty miles up Highway 88 and would spend vacations and holidays working on his "little cabin". One Sunday after morning church service, Albert insisted that I ride up the mountain with him so he could show me his project.

"Now Albert, you are not a mountain man," warned Brother Ball, "and those mountains can be dangerous this time of year."

"My Scout can go anywhere, at any time."

Albert had an International Scout vehicle with four wheel drive that obviously gave him a lot of confidence in his driving skills. I, on the other hand, was apprehensive and really did not want to risk getting stuck in the deep snow, so I reminded Albert that evening services started at 7:00 and said I did not think we would be able to make it back in time. But he insisted and I gave in—partly because I wanted to see the cabin, but mostly because I didn't want to keep saying no.

Albert and I started the climb on Highway 88, and within 15 miles it started to snow. The higher we traveled, the harder it snowed. I noticed that we had not passed another vehicle in some time.

"Albert, this is far enough; you need to turn around and go back."

He would not listen, and after several more miles we were "high centered" in the snow. We were stuck. In other words, his four wheel drive meant nothing in our current situation. We got out and tried digging the snow away from the wheels, but even if we got them free, there was no place to turn around. The time was now 5:00pm, and I knew June would have started being concerned. We waited in the freezing cold for two more hours for someone to drive by and see us, but I knew the chances of that were getting smaller the lower the sun set. It looked as if we were the only stupid travelers in that area.

"Albert, unless God sends some help really soon, we are going to die in these mountains, and it is your fault."

He got out of the vehicle and tried to tie his wench to some object off the road while I prayed. As I closed my prayer, I looked up and in the distance I saw two Jeeps with huge balloon tires. I waved frantically at them, and they turned their vehicles in our direction. Our rescuers were local West Point young men. They explained that they were up in the heavy snow playing around, but in pairs in the event one of them was to get into trouble. They recognized me right away.

"Preacher, what in the world are you doing up here in that inadequate vehicle?"

I admitted to my foolishness without looking at Albert. The Jeeps pulled us free, turned us around, and followed us down to a level that we could travel safely on our own.

Trying to keep the edginess out of my voice, but wanting to make a point, I said to Albert, "I hope you realize that were it not for God's intervention, we would have been dead."

He replied, "That old Scout of mine would have gotten us out."

As I had expected, June was frantic by the time we got back to West Point. She was so mad at Albert that she said she was tempted to tell him how stupid it was for him to drag me up there. Thankfully, my irritation had subsided by then, and I was able to remind her that I was equally, if not more, responsible for my brush with death. I, the stupid city boy, had underestimated the dangers of mountain travel; the snowy peaks are indeed beautiful, but they can be very dangerous if you do not have a proper respect for them. I also learned that it is sometimes better to risk a friendship and say no than to give in to pressure just so the other person won't be upset.

## Out of the Mouth of Babes

To my dismay, Martha's and Ron's divorce was final. But Martha embraced us and we were delighted to have her and the girls in our daily lives. I was able to teach the girls so many things I thought were important as we spent hours together talking, reading, playing, and praying. My granddaughters were great prayer warriors. Glenda was known to round up all the family, sometimes several times a day, and tell us it was time for us to pray. We took turns, but Tracy was always ready and willing and could say the cutest things. June and I would often have to stifle our giggles. It seemed to take Terri the longest because she prayed about everything; my hurt elbow, Grandma Marie's broken collarbone, the dirty dishes in the sink . . . you get the picture.

One day, I had returned from seminary, and Terri was in the bedroom with my one volume encyclopedia looking at the pictures as she turned the pages. She did not know I was watching her from the hallway. She would turn a page and if she saw a Viking ship, for instance, her comment would be, "Jesus, I didn't know you had a boat." She never knew I was outside the door laughing with pure joy. She just kept on turning the pages and talking to Jesus about everything she saw. She was about three at the time.

## No Small Thing

It was within my first month at seminary that I failed a test covering the 400 year period between the Old and New Testaments. Dumbfounded, I was talking to myself, out loud, as I walked down the steps staring at the big, red 'F' at the top of my paper.

"If I could just find one man on this campus that is as thick-skulled as I am, I would feel a whole lot better."

Just then, someone on the step behind me tapped me on the shoulder.

"I am your man; I just failed the same test!"

We both laughed, and immediately the depressing reality of academic requirements seemed less ominous—I was in good company. In 1970, I graduated from Seminary with a Diploma in Theology. June was awarded an "IPHT" diploma, which means, I Put Him Through. The graduation services were beautiful. My family was all there. My mother bought my class ring which is still one of my prized possessions.

My church was a member of the Mother Lode Association, a group of eight churches scattered within a radius of 100 miles. All eight churches were small congregations like ours. When the time came for our quarterly association meeting to be held in First Baptist of Jackson, California, the weather was cold and snowy. Only three pastors and six church members were in attendance, and the nine of us were sitting around a wood stove trying to keep warm, feeling very sorry for ourselves, and bemoaning how hard it was to pastor in such small church organizations. In the middle of our pity party, a stranger walked into the meeting and introduced himself as the Director of Missions for the Southern Baptist Convention of California. He expressed his gratitude for our generous support of the state convention and spoke encouragingly about our role in the bigger picture. I immediately felt embarrassed by my attitude just minutes before he arrived.

I never again felt slighted by pastoring a small church. I realized that there is no small work in God's kingdom. I decided not only to stay at West Point, but to move June and myself there. Brother Ball and the congregation were very surprised because they had assumed that I would move on to a larger church following graduation, but they were elated, and the members came to San Anselmo to help us with the move. The church had purchased a small, two bedroom home in the adjoining community of Wilseyville, California. The parsonage even had a building on the back of the property that was ideally suited for my workshop and office space.

---

June and I were very pleased with all the details of this next step except for one; Martha had decided to take Glenda, Tracy and Terri and move back to Texas to live with her mother. Oh how we missed her and the girls. We had them with us for so many years; they were like our own children.

---

Wilseyville was such a beautiful place. There was a creek called Middle Fork where all the kids went swimming in the summer during the heat of the day. Much to my pleasure, I was asked to join them, but I quickly expressed my great dislike of cold water.

"Aw it's not cold. Come on in!" they coaxed.

I'm not sure what came over me, but I dove in head first. As I hit the clear surface, I was immediately reminded of exactly where this water originates . . . it's melted snow, of course, from the mountains, so it is FREEZING! It was bearable only after I'd been in it for about fifteen minutes, and all of my extremities were numb.

Glenda and Tracy spent time with June and me during the summers we were in Wilseyville, and we shared many adventures when they were there. They were all flourishing: Glenda was twelve, trying to be more like fifteen, and fit in nicely with the local teen aged kids, Tracy was nine, acting accordingly. Terri was six—too young to be away from her mother for so long—so she stayed in Odessa while her sisters visited us in California.

One day, I took Glenda and Tracy to a commercial fishing pond. The fish there would almost fight to get on your hook, and I was looking forward to watching all the excitement. Tracy's long hair kept getting caught in the reel, slowing her down. Nonetheless, the fishing was so successful that I had to stop the process after about an hour or risk going broke. The pond management cleaned the catch and charged by the pound. On the way home, I recited a little poem.

"Little fishy in the brook,

Pap-Paw caught him with a hook,

Mam-Maw fried him in a pan and

Tracy ate him like a man."

(Tracy loved the poem so much she recited it over and over until Glenda pleaded for her to stop.)

> Tracy spent most of her time reading—she loved it. One summer she read every fourth grade book in the public library.

## What Comes Around

Tempress Industries, the company I had been setting the diamonds for, advised me that they were going to start doing this step themselves, and I would no longer be needed. Soon after, one of their engineers came to West Point to visit me and asked if I would be willing to tell them how I set the diamonds. I was not inclined to share my process with them and my answer was no. The engineer went back empty handed, and I assume they began the difficult task of developing their own methods. This left me without a substantial portion of my income. I still received fifty dollars a week from the church, but we were running through our savings fairly quickly. I petitioned the Home Mission Board for some help, and I was granted a small salary. The additional funds were welcomed, but the bigger payoff was being classified as a home missionary and having my name on that prayer list. What a blessing it was to have millions of Baptists from all over the world praying for me!

For the next year I was able to devote myself full-time to the church, but the church wasn't able to pay me a full-time salary. Our savings were completely depleted by then, and I prayed for what to do next. There were some openings in the timber industry, but I was not qualified to do that kind of work. I made a trip to Sunnyvale, California, and called on Tempress Industries. The company had been purchased by Lynden Furnace Company. The products were the same, just under different management. I applied for a job, and because of my background and experience, I was hired as a production supervisor in the diamond scribing tool department. I kept my pastorate in West Point, but June and I moved to San Jose to be close to the manufacturing plant where I would be employed. Once again, we found ourselves driving the 300 miles round trip to the church field. We would leave San Jose on Friday after I got off work and return home Sunday night.

My duties at the plant included supervising fifteen women in the manufacture of diamond scribing tools and involved setting and polishing the diamonds on lapping machines. The company was shipping 4000 diamond scribing tools per month, but their diamond setting process was terrible, and complaints were coming in from the field about the inferiority of the product. On one occasion, I was called into quality control to look at some returned diamond scribers. The customers and salesmen had returned several hundred tools, and they were being re-inspected. I was asked what I thought about the diamonds.

"They are of such poor quality that they are little more than junk."

The plant superintendent replied, "I don't care, ship all you can make and sell."

Although I was the expert, no one seemed to listen to my warnings. I knew that I was not going to last long under these conditions, having no option but to do things their way, but I felt like I was between a rock and a hard place with nowhere to turn.

Sometime later, a man named Jim Loomis called me at work and invited me to lunch. We went to a local restaurant, and Jim began telling me about himself. He was once employed by Tempress as a sales engineer, but clashed with management over the lack of testing facilities and overall poor product quality. He had left the company and planned to design a new type of diamond scriber. Someone had given him my name as an expert in the selecting and mounting of small diamonds. (To this day I do not know who gave him my name.)

Jim and I instantly had a liking for each other.

"Les, if I get this product going, would you consider mounting the diamonds for me?"

"I will certainly pray about it."

"By the way Les, don't be surprised if you get called into the office when you go back to work, because several of my ex-bosses are in this restaurant having lunch."

I looked around, and he was right. After lunch I returned to work, and just like Jim said, I was called to the office. My employer asked me to have a seat.

"Les are you happy here with us?"

"Yes I am, basically, but no one seems to pay me or my ideas much attention."

My employer smiled. "You know, Les, you are long overdue for a raise. I am going to see that your salary is increased, and your ideas are at least noted."

Things did indeed change for the better. The engineer that dismissed my ideas was fired, and my compensation was increased substantially. The next time I saw Jim Loomis I thanked him for the raise! He laughed and vowed to me that within a year he would be making me an offer.

## Best Laid Plans

I saw my son only twice the following year. He came to visit us because I was so loaded down with work and could not get off to go to him. I could see the damage the drinking and drug use was doing, and there seemed to be nothing I could do about it except pray. Prayer is a powerful weapon, and I knew that someday there would be victory. As I watched him leave from West Point to return to Southern California, I cannot begin to tell you of the heartache as memories flooded my soul. I have learned that memories should be treasured and never forgotten. As I write this book I am flooded with memories. If I recorded all my memories, this book would have to be three times the size. Just my times with my granddaughters alone would fill half the book. June and I remember all their little ways of saying certain words, and of the many times at play with them. They have heard all my stories, and I have been accused of making some of them up, but they are all absolutely true.

During the 1970's, an oil embargo was placed on America by OPEC creating a shortage of gasoline like this nation had not experienced since WWII. Prices soared to one dollar a gallon, cars lined up around the block to get gas, tempers flared at the pumps, and there were reported fist fights among customers. Rationing using odd and even days for buying gasoline was tried with some success. Having to drive the 300 miles round trip to my church field quicly became more problematic; I self-rationed my fuel usage as best I could.

One Friday when I got off work, I was only able to get one half a tank of gas, which was sufficient to get me to West Point but not enough to get me back to San Jose. June and I prayed about whether to attempt the trip home. We both heard God telling us to go, so we set off. We left West Point after the evening service and headed home knowing we had to find gas along the way. Every station we passed had signs reading **"NO GAS"**. June kept on praying.

Our gas gauge was on empty as we approached a modest grocery store that had one gasoline pump. They had turned off all their lights, and were in the process of closing. I pulled into the station, got out of the car, and went to the door and knocked. The owner opened the door, and I told him my story.

He said, "Sir, I have a full container of gasoline. People have been driving right by here all day and not stopping. I guess I am a little out of the way for most travelers, but you can have all the gas you want."

As I was pumping the gas, I could hear the relief in June's voice as she thanked God for his provision and we continued that prayer of thanks all the way home.

---

"Get up and go, and I will go with you." God

---

The trips to West Point were a pleasant time for June and me to visit about our week and to discuss the upcoming weekend, but the trips home from the church field were becoming increasingly difficult for me. Many times on the way home, I would have to stop and take a ten or fifteen minute nap while June patiently waited. She became a skilled coffee-pourer and could get the contents of a thermos bottle into a cup without losing a drop given any road condition. The caffeine helped, but I would be so tired by the time we reached home I could hardly move. I had been making this trip six years. I was on my third automobile. The old Buick was still with Martha. The 1967 Ford had worn out, and the 1970 Ford I had was close to failure. Mountain driving tore up tires very fast; ten thousand miles was about all I could get out of a set. I tried retreads and new tires, but the life was about the same.

I awoke on most Monday mornings still completely exhausted. It was painfully obvious that I had reached my own physical limitations. One particular morning, on my way to work, I was especially down. I was having my morning prayer in the car—I have had some of my best prayers while driving—and I implored God. "Lord, you know my heart, and I don't want to leave the church at West Point, but I just cannot physically do this anymore. Would you please open up the doors to a full-time church, or in some way change my present situation?"

I came home from work that very same day, and there was a letter from Gene Lake, the Area Missionary over the Crescent Bay, West Los Angeles Baptist Association. Mr. Lake introduced himself in the letter and asked me to send him a resume. There were several churches in his area without pastors. I thanked the Lord and sent my resume. Remember this letter from Mr. Lake, because it will be referred to as this book progresses. I assumed God was going to make some changes very shortly, so the drive to West Point seemed a little less stressful.

Then I heard from Jim Loomis who was very excited because he was on the verge of getting his diamond scriber products on the market. He had great plans. "Les, when I get this thing going, you can move back to West Point, and we will set up the diamond setting end of the business there. We will both prosper from this arrangement." This would be ideal for me; I could live on the church field, and make good money while doing it. I loved the church, and I thought all my problems were solved. I advised Jim to go ahead with his plans and that I was ready to commit as soon as he was ready to go.

Before long, I received a call from Mr. Tracy Ware, Chairman of the Pulpit Committee at Calvary Baptist Church in Hawthorne, California. I assumed it was in response to the resume I had previously submitted to Mr. Lake. He asked me if I would mail him a cassette tape of one of my recent sermons. I taped the next Sunday morning service and sent him a copy. The next week, Tracy called and asked if I would be willing to come to the church and preach for them so that the congregation could hear my message in person and meet me afterwards. June and I accepted the invitation and traveled to Hawthorne the following week.

> I was especially anxious to go to Hawthorne because Ron was living in the same area, and I knew I would get to see him again.

It was difficult to hide my disappointment as we drove onto the church property; the buildings were ugly, grass was growing through the asphalt parking lot, and the whole place looked rundown. The church had gone through a split, and there were only about twenty people there that Sunday to hear me preach. After the morning service, I met with the pulpit committee, and they advised me that in approximately three months—the time it would take to sell one piece of church property and pay off their entire mortgage—they would be ready to call a full-time pastor. Their intent was to make me an offer at that time. I told them that June and I would pray about it.

I wanted so much for the deal with Jim Loomis to go through. I did not want to pastor that church; I wanted to set diamonds for Jim Loomis and pastor at West Point.

"This is great," I said to June, "it is going to take Calvary Baptist Church several months to prepare for a full-time pastor, and in the meantime, Jim will be ready for me, and we will be in the money. Come on Jim!" A little greed had entered my heart, and to appease my guilt, I made a bargain with God. I knew full well that making bargains with God wasn't wise, but I was so sure Jim Loomis would make an offer long before the church was ready to call me that my boldness got the best of me.

"Lord whichever one makes the first offer, Loomis or Calvary Baptist, will decide for me which is right. Lord, you just take care of it."

I was certain Loomis would be the answer; however, the following week, I received a call from Calvary Baptist that the church had sold the property much quicker than they had anticipated and that the full-time position was available immediately. I was asked to come the following Sunday in view of a call as pastor. I reluctantly agreed.

"Les," I asked myself, "you knowingly and willingly bargained with God. Now what are you going to do?"

I showed up as agreed, but with an attitude of resignation and a hope that the elders would not make me an offer.

On the way home, June and I decided to take the new Interstate 5 Freeway. The highway had just opened and the service stations were few and far between, but we had a full tank and decided the change of scenery would do us good. We were on a long vacant stretch of road when our car started running hot. I pulled off on the shoulder, parked the car, raised the hood, and began looking for the problem. A radiator hose had split, and we had lost all of our water. I scanned the horizon so I could wave down the next motorist to pass by, and there was no help in sight. We were stranded.

My prayer warrior wife was always the voice of reason. "Kessler, we had better pray."

We bowed our heads, and prayed with all our might. We closed our prayer, and when we looked up, there was a Highway Patrol car parked down the road about three hundred yards. I suppose the officers had pulled up and stopped to observe us. They turned on their lights and came toward us. After I explained our situation, a wrecker was radioed, and within thirty minutes we had been towed to the nearest town. Necessary repairs were made, and we were back on our way in a very short time.

A few days later, Tracy Ware called and said the church had voted unanimously to call me as their pastor. They needed an answer from me, and if I accepted the call, I was asked to be on the church field in three weeks. As June and I left for West Point that Friday, I knew I had to make a decision as soon as possible. For the entire 150 mile drive to West Point, I went backwards and forwards over all the practical reasons why I should turn them down and wait for Jim Loomis' offer. June just let me talk. She knew the bargain I had made with God. As soon as we got to West Point, I picked up the phone with the intention of declining, but I just could not do it—I could not get my own words out of my head.

"Lord whoever makes the offer first; I will accept that as your choice."

I accepted the church's offer. The great relief I experienced was almost immediate, and I have never been sorry for the decision. Apparently, June was never in doubt.

"Kessler, I listened to you jabber about all the reasons you would not take the church. I knew very well that you were going to accept because I knew the stupid bargain you had made with God."

I resigned from my pastorate in West Point after almost eight years of service, and resigned my job with Lynden Furnace Company. The church located a home for us in Inglewood that was within our budget and managed by a wonderful landlord that seemed genuinely happy to have us.

My son and his friend Bruce offered to come to San Jose to pack everything and move it to our new home. I tried to help, but I just got in their way. Bruce had been in the moving business before and seemed to know exactly what he was doing. I, obviously, did not.

"Dad, why don't you just stay in the house with mom?"

I didn't need to be asked twice. They loaded up the large U-Haul truck in no time, and we made our move to the new church. Several men from the church helped Ron and Bruce unload, and in short order, June had us up and running.

It was a joy to be living in the same area as Ron, and we began to see much more of each other. I met my very pretty fourth granddaughter, Ronda, who was now about five years old and a little shy at first. But after just a few visits, she showed herself to be a typical, energy filled, loving child.

# 1973-1983

## A Solid Start

I began my pastorate at Calvary Baptist Church in 1974; there was much work to be done. My first Sunday on the field, Varney Bancroft, the church treasurer, asked to see me. "Pastor, during the church split the congregation quit giving to the church and began sending all their offerings to various TV evangelists."

I decided that I would correct the problem or get fired trying. As I began to develop the sermon for the next Sunday on New Testament giving, I decided it would be helpful to browse the local Christian bookstore for relevant material. I came upon a small book written by a Methodist minister. The title caught my eye—"Oral Roberts Won't Do Your Funeral". In it, the author described the ill effects that televangelists were having on small churches across the country. I read the book from cover to cover and sympathized with this pastor's plight. I was so moved that I borrowed the title of the book for my sermon, used its contents to educate my congregation, and prayed that they would gain understanding. The church responded with more positive feedback than I could have dreamed of receiving, I was not asked to leave immediately, and giving increased consistently from that day forward.

We formed a choir and, in a short amount of time, had funds available to call a music director, youth director, and a choir director. As our numbers began to steadily grow, a youth ministry and a children's ministry were created. We remodeled the church and repaved the parking lot. I served as Stewardship Chairman with the Crescent Bay, West Los Angeles Association, and later, I served on the Executive Board of the Southern Baptist Convention of California. We also had a pastors' breakfast meeting the first Tuesday of each month. I enjoyed my pastorate and learned a great deal about denominational responsibilities. The congregation treated June and me like family, and they made themselves available to us whenever we had need.

> The ladies of the church had such wonderful cooking skills that we became famous for our southern potluck dinners.

# Diversification

Jim Loomis contacted me to let me know that he had created a very small budget for diamond mounting and asked if I could help him. I had a small garage at the house we were renting, so I set up my equipment and began to mount a small number of diamonds for him. I would mount the diamonds for him, and send him an invoice, but Jim was struggling to get started.

"I promise that I will pay you when I can."

"Jim, don't worry about it, just get your product going, I am making it alright on my church salary."

> For over twenty years, Jim and I conducted business without ever requiring contracts or purchase orders.

We got together in San Francisco some time later, and Jim confessed that he and his wife had gone through a heartbreaking divorce, that he had given her their home (which represented about ninety percent of their assets), and that he had kept only the struggling little business. He was renting a room from some friends and working non-stop to get his business going. I felt such sorrow for all that he had been through. Jim Loomis was the epitome of courage, and I told him as much.

June and I were doing alright, but our budget was tight and getting tighter. Thankfully, the church was able to give us a raise, which definitely helped, and I was able to officiate at weddings to supplement our income. One morning after services, I was approached by a lady in our church, Mary C., who owned a wedding chapel in Inglewood, a very short distance from Hawthorne. Mary had several in-house clergymen during the week to perform the ceremonies for her, but she needed someone for Saturdays—her biggest day. I accepted. I hated to give up my only day off, but we needed the extra money. I would begin as early as nine in the morning and finish as late as nine in the evening with very few breaks in between. I was paid ten dollars per event from Mary and sometimes there were tips from the wedding party.

It was a good experience. I learned about wedding planning and rehearsals, and even developed some good wedding themes. I was fairly flexible depending upon the situation. Mary operated her business on a Christian basis. Alcoholic beverages were prohibited at the receptions, and Mary was usually very ethical in her business practices. She did a great job budgeting time and expenses and conformed to California laws, usually getting all the paper work done before the wedding started The wedding chapel had a beautiful garden courtyard and, unless the weather didn't cooperate, most weddings took place outside.

I did not realize it at the time, but the minute I signed my name to that document, the couple was considered legally married.

**The clergyman's point of view.** Very few wedding parties care much about what the minister thinks, but I have observed a few things: Weddings are the bride's day. She should have everything her way (it may be the last time). Mothers of the brides their daughters, many think they should do most of the planning, and are unaware of the distress they cause their daughters. For instance, the wedding dress reflects the bride's personality, and should be exactly what the bride selects. Sometimes, mothers clash with their daughters and want more say in the selection. Fathers are unique individuals. It kills them to lose their little girls, and they are usually the ones footing most of the bill. They just want their little girls to be happy.

## All Weddings Aren't Created Equal

Although I felt that performing marriage ceremonies was an important part of my ministry, there were a few I did not enjoy—to say the least. One such wedding was a four party wedding. The bride's brother acted as best man and the groom's sister acted as the maid of honor. From the very beginning, the group was unruly and irreverent. They laughed at everything spiritual I had to say and made jokes to each other during the ceremony. I did the best I could to hold my temper. I stopped talking mid-sentence when they made light of my words, but they didn't seem to notice. It got so bad that finally the best man spoke up.

"Come on guys, cool it or we will never get through this thing."

The disrespect continued, so I just abruptly completed the ceremony.

"By the authority vested in me, and complying with the laws of the state of California, I pronounce you to be husband and wife."

The bride asked, "But what about the rings?"

I said, "Put them on and wear them."

I walked away and left them standing there.

Mary mentioned later that the bride made a comment to her about the incident, "I think we made the reverend angry".

On another occasion, Mary asked me to do a special cliff side, ocean view wedding in Palos Verdes, California. The wedding was to be at four in the afternoon that coming Saturday. Since I was not familiar with that area, I left at noon so I would be early. When I arrived at the spot I found on the map, there was no cliff side at all. Where was I?

The harder I tried, the more lost I became. I finally stopped at a phone booth to call Mary. I had a coin, but of all times, I did not have a pen in my pocket to write anything down. I am a preacher, and you will never find me without a pen. I walked next door to a stop-and-go type store, went in, and looked for a pen to buy—there is always an abundance of ball point pens for sale. Not here. I asked the clerk if he had any pencils for sale. He responded that all he had was the pencil he was using. I offered him a dollar for it. He broke it in half and sold me the sharpened end. I went back to the phone booth and called Mary. "Where are you? The wedding party has been calling me non-stop."

I said, "Mary, I am lost.".

I called the number she gave me, and the bride's father answered. I explained to him that I was lost, told him there were no cliffs in sight, and gave him the name of the street I was currently on.

"Man, you are at the other end of the peninsula!"

Apparently, the two streets I was looking for on my map cross each other at both ends of the peninsula. I was simply at the wrong end. And now in a panic—I did not have much daylight left—I still had a long way to go. I got lost again, and called the bride's father a second time.

He answered. "Reverend, where are you right now?"

"I am parked in front of a fire station, next to a liquor store."

"Stay right there. I am only ten minutes from you. I will come and get you and lead you to the wedding. I am a gray-haired man, and I will be driving a red Jaguar."

Ten minutes later, a red Jaguar convertible drove up with a woman in the passenger seat and a gray-haired man at the wheel. I hurried up to the car, obviously flustered.

"Do you want me to follow you?"

The man replied, "Who in the world are you?" and drove off in a hurry.

Five minutes later, another red Jaguar drove up with a gray-haired man at the wheel, and this time I stood there and didn't move. The man rolled down the window.

"Are you the Reverend? Please follow me!"

When we arrived at the wedding site, the sun was already going down, and the bride was having a tantrum. Who could blame her? I pulled out the necessary paperwork so we could quickly get all the signing done before we began. I still did not have a pen. The bride turned to the audience.

"The Reverend does not have a pen; can someone *please* lend him a pen?"

The ceremony began. The best man held a flashlight while the bride and groom, who had written their own vows, read theirs to each other. The hired photographer continued to take pictures though, by now, it was completely dark. I did not get a tip, and left as quickly as I could. It was amazing how the darkness changed how everything looked and how easy it was to lose my way again. I knew

June would be worried by now, so I stopped at another phone booth (oh, how easy it would have been if cell phones had been available in those days!). As I began to explain to June what had happened, the humor of it all hit me, and I started to laugh. It must have been catching or maybe she was relieved to know I hadn't fallen off the cliff, but either way, June laughed, too, and it was several minutes before we could stop.

The bride immediately sued Mary for $3000.00 in damages to compensate her for the botched wedding. Mary asked me to accompany her to court.

"Why do I need to be there? Haven't I done enough damage?"

She finally convinced me to go on her behalf. The plaintiff brought all her ruined pictures and described her unhappiness with the wedding. I was then asked to tell my side of the story, and to the best of my ability, I told the judge everything—even about the two red Jaguars. (I think he wanted to laugh but couldn't.) The ruling was in favor of the plaintiff for the sum of $1000, but the judge was a fair man, and I appreciated his closing statement.

"As far as I am concerned, you both owe the Reverend an apology. You sent this man into a strange area with only cross streets as a reference."

Needless to say, I became concerned about doing weddings for Mary, and I was tired of feeling manipulated. I advised Mary that she should be looking for someone else, but that I would continue until she found a replacement.

The last wedding I performed for Mary made the National Enquirer magazine.

Mary had called me at home late one weekday evening. "Brother Les, can you come do a very important wedding for me? None of my ministers are available; can you come help me just this once?"

I agreed and rushed to the chapel; there were men with cameras and note pads everywhere. I was introduced to the bride to be. She was a beautiful woman, immaculately attired in a breathtaking dress. She was also charming, and the camera men around her were obviously impressed.

"Isn't she beautiful for a sixty year old woman?"

I signed the marriage license as did both witnesses. I was then directed to the groom's lounge in the garden where the ceremony was to take place. On my way to the lounge, one of the men with a camera introduced himself as being with the National Enquirer magazine and asked if he could interview me. Based on my knowledge of this magazine, I declined. I opened the door to the groom's lounge and saw a young man about twenty years old sitting there.

"Where is the groom?"

"I am the groom," he replied.

I would not have chosen to do the ceremony had I been given more information, but I had already signed the marriage license, and this couple was legally married. I did what I had come to do and left as quickly as I could.

At a deacons meeting the following Sunday, I relayed the story to the group, and they laughed hysterically. "Les, haven't you been reading the papers? The bride and groom were from England, and could not get married there because the woman had once been married to the groom's father or grandfather. Even though they were not related by blood line, the Church of England would not do the ceremony, so the couple came to America."

I insisted on my ignorance of the matter, but my friends gave me a good ribbing. The following month, National Enquirer had a front page picture of the wedding party. Thank goodness, the photo was taken from the rear, and all that was shown of me was the back of my head. I must have a very distinct look from the back of my head, because a lot of people still recognized me. I got teased a lot, and although I never lived the event down, I did have a standard comeback.

"When was the last time you made the National Enquirer?"

My ministry at Calvary Baptist was so satisfying to me. I had developed a large children's ministry and was preaching children's sermons to about 100–120 children each Sunday. We had called Chris Post as music and youth director, and I was actively involved with all the youth. A lot of the families were into dirt biking and kept insisting that I go with them. I explained that I loved motorcycles and rode one all through college; however, it had been years since I had ridden and I did not have dirt bike to ride. They insisted on me using a spare they had. I reluctantly went with them and became an instant addict to off road riding, continuing to ride until 2013, just shy of my 90th birthday. Dirt biking is a wonderful sport, exercises every bone in your body and unwinds your pressures like no other. Serious injuries seem to come when you ride above your abilities. I never did that because I was taught by excellent riders who stressed safety and sanity.

## Second (and Third) Chances

My son called me.

"Dad, I have a lady friend I would like for you and mom to meet."

I said alright, but I was a little skeptical since I had not cared much for the previous lady. Ron brought Pam McCollum to meet us, and I was immediately impressed. I would guess that Pam had never met anyone who did not instantly like her. She was a teetotaler—did not drink alcohol—and although she did not condone his behavior, she loved Ron unconditionally. Unfortunately, Ron was still drinking heavily and doing drugs, but he still looked handsome.

Ron and Pam were living together. Pam was an excellent cook, but didn't eat very much in her constant battle with her weight. She prepared many meals that Ron failed to show up for because he would be who-knows-where, too intoxicated to get home. Many times she had to go pick him up. Pam was very patient with Ron; she was not a nag. And she never complained. She just loved Ron with an unconditional love.

> Ron and Pam were married in 1981, and I was privileged to do the wedding in a friend's home. The union did not stop Ron's drinking and drug use, but Pam refused to let it get her down. She had a true heart for her family: my son Ron, her little boy Jason, her mother Margaret, her sister, her two brothers, my wife June, and me.

Ron was driving drunk on a Los Angeles freeway. He lost control of the car on an overpass and plunged down the embankment. The vehicle landed so hard that all four wheels were crushed into a horizontal position. The car was smashed and a tree limb had come through the window on the passenger side at an angle, passed right over the steering wheel, and exited out the rear of the car on the driver's side. Ron did not have on a seat belt and was thrown to the floorboard on the passenger side. The police had to call for the jaws-of-life to extricate Ron from the wreckage. The only injuries my son received were a broken nose and some pieces of glass embedded in his face. It was truly a miracle. By all rights, no one should be able to live through a wreck like that. If Ron's seat belt had been fastened, the tree would have decapitated him. That should have been enough for my son to seek sobriety, but it was not.

> I want to make it clear at this point that my son was never a bad person; he just made bad choices in life. Ron was still the likeable person he had always been and our deep love for him never faded, but I knew that the lifestyle he was living would cause terrible consequences. All the problems caught up with him all at once.

Again, Ron was driving his cement truck under the influence of both alcohol and drugs. He was caught going the wrong way on a Los Angeles freeway and was taken to jail. He woke up among all the other drunks and had no memory of how he got there. This was serious. Our family doctor came to his court date and suggested to the judge that Ron could benefit from a three month rehabilitation program in Long Beach. Ron's license was suspended, and he was allowed to enter the program in Long Beach with severe warnings that there would be no leniency for subsequent charges.

During the program, Ron met a young man whose sister owned a Trucking Company. Alice was a hard-nosed individual who put up with no nonsense and was capable of holding her own with any man or woman. She agreed to see Ron when he completed the program. Ron graduated from the program sober and remorseful. He realized how his life was in ruins.

> After putting up with his addictions for many years, Pam finally had a sober husband. I am very happy to say at the writing of this book that Ron has been sober and drug free for over 30 years. I am still encouraging him to join AA and attend their meetings—those poor alcoholics need to hear that someone can be clean for 30 years.

Alice interviewed Ron, and she decided to give him a job but would tolerate no mess ups. Just a single incident would be grounds for termination. Driving a freight truck was hard, but at that time, it was exactly what Ron needed. His license was still suspended except for work, so Pam drove him to work and back. I had the opportunity to meet Alice, and when I did, I expressed how grateful I was that she was willing to give my son a second chance. Ron became one of her most dependable and trusted drivers and, on one of my visits, she gave him an easy run and allowed me to go with him. I came to respect the skills of a truck driver as I witnessed first-hand some of the dumb mistakes automobile drivers make. For one thing, many drivers do not realize how long it takes to get a big rig to stop, and they carelessly zip in front of one at a light—filling in the safety cushion the driver has created for himself. And it seems they don't know or care about how many near collisions they cause when they impatiently hurry to get around the rigs.

## Trick and Treat

June's mother had a stroke, and June decided to make a trip to Texas to be with her for a month. The church was very supportive and took good care of me while June was gone. I never ate so well in all my life. Now, I mentioned that we had great cooks in the church. I was almost to the point of taking reservations for the many dinner invitations I was receiving. Each Sunday morning I would brag on the most recent provision, and it almost became a contest between families as to who could come up with the most sumptuous meals. I must have gained ten pounds. I relied on my bachelor tricks to get me through as well—these I shared with the congregation, much to their amusement. I would sleep on the left side of the bed one week and on the right side the next to save on changing the sheets. I washed shorts and socks in the shower each night. When June returned, she was amazed at how well I got along without her, and was thankful that the church had taken such good care of her husband.

## It's Never Too Late

While at Calvary, I discovered that I had a God-given compassion for dying folks. It seemed that there was at least one terminal patient per month for the many years I ministered there, and I led many to a saving knowledge of Jesus before they passed away. I knew God was using me in a special way, and each death bed confession remains indelible on my memory. One in particular was very unusual. My deacon and treasurer, Varney B., asked if I would be willing to go with him to see his brother-in-law who was terminally ill in the hospital and had only weeks to live.

"Of course I will go with you," I replied. "Just tell me when."

Varney said, "As soon as possible, but I must warn you that he is a church hater, despises preachers, and has refused to let the hospital chaplain counsel with him. Do not be surprised if he is rude or curses you. He is very, very bitter."

"Don't worry," I replied, and the next night Varney and I went to see his brother-in-law.

We entered John's room and Varney introduced me as his pastor. John immediately began crying, and grabbed me by the hand.

"I was hoping someone would come that could tell me how to find peace with God."

I explained God's love and quoted 1 John 1:9, "If we confess our sins, He is faithful and just to forgive us of our sins, and cleanse us of all unrighteousness." I had a prayer of faith with him, and he sweetly gave his life to Jesus. A week later, Varney told me how happy John had become and seemed to be at peace.

He said to Varney, "I know my soul is secure with God, and I would be totally at peace if I could just take communion before I die. Do you think it would be possible?"

Varney let me know John's desire, and I called a special deacon's meeting and informed them of the request. They were all in favor of taking the elements of the Lord's Supper to John at the hospital and conducting a special service. Two weeks later he died. I know some Christians do not believe in "death bed confessions", but I do. I believe that God wants a soul so badly that if the soul is willing, God will reach out to him until the very minute death comes. I have observed too many glorious conversions to have any doubts whatsoever.

> Pam's mother developed lung cancer, and I had the privilege of reading the Bible to her and inviting her to become a Christian. She was so happy the night she truly believed that God had forgiven all her past sins and had a place for her in heaven. Margaret died a very contented woman.

## Things Can and Do Change in an Instant

My mother had managed an apartment building for years, and I thought she was doing just fine; however, early in 1979, the owner of the building called me to let me know of his concerns for my mother's health. I made a trip to Houston and was amazed at how much my mother had declined mentally and physically in just the one year since I'd seen her last. I decided that my mother could no longer live alone, and I moved her to California. I had grossly underestimated the trauma an elderly person goes through when they are moved away from familiar surroundings, and things were just not working.

In addition, June's mother had gotten worse, and my dad was having mental problems to the extent that, if they continued to worsen, he would not be able to live alone either. My mother was miserable, June's mother was in decline, and my father would soon need help. I turned to the Lord and another miracle happened.

I was on the phone speaking to Marshall Hayes Jr. in Houston, Texas about some tools he needed. "Oh, by the way Les, Dad said the next time I talked to you to let him know he wants to ask you something,"

He put his dad on the line.

"Les", Mr. Hayes said, "I have been praying about you, and God has convinced me it is time for you to move back to Houston. I do not know what your situation is, but I definitely feel that you should move here and manage my diamond tool manufacturing business. I will move you to Texas. I know you make specialty diamond tools for the semiconductor industry in your own shop, and as long as it does not interfere with your work for me, you can keep on doing it. I know you are a pastor, and would take some church here, but I will build the shop around your pastoral ministry. I believe you can handle it."

I replied, "You don't realize what a miracle just happened. I do need to move to Texas because all our parents are getting old and cannot care for themselves, but I just did not know how I could afford to do it."

We discussed salary, came to a figure, and I accepted with joy. I resigned my pastorate at Calvary Baptist Church. It was a very sad time for me, my friends, and our congregation, but once the people realized my situation, they were supportive and happy for me and my family.

Industrial Diamond Products moved us bag and baggage to Houston. I bought a house in Jacinto City to be near June's mother and father who had been able to arrange for full-time help in their home. I placed my mother into a nursing facility near us, and my dad was content knowing that he would be moved into his sister's home with her when the time came. At last we had our parents fairly well situated. Martha had moved to Houston with the children prior to our relocation there, and we were delighted to be living in the same city as our darling granddaughters again. June and I joined Mason Drive Baptist Church where my father attended. Pastor Ash knew that I was searching for a pastorate, and he began sending my résumé to the various churches that he knew were searching for pastors.

I started my job at Industrial Diamond Products the week after we arrived in Houston. I was early the first day, and there was no one there, though everybody began coming in shortly. I got along very well with both the office and shop personnel. I loved the job. It was challenging. Business was booming.

Marshall Hayes called me into his office. "Les, the shop is yours. Go make me some money."

What a great relationship had developed between us through the years. I know God shut the door the first time I was offered a job by Marshall because the time was not right. Now twenty-something years later the door opened.

---

I had many great experiences at Industrial Diamond Products, as well as some heartache. Marshall developed liver cancer and passed away. I grieved for my friend, and I will always cherish the memories and be indebted to him for his hand in my life.

---

In July of 1981 I received a phone call from an interim pastor at Roslyn Baptist Church asking me to come and preach for them the next Sunday. As I drove into the parking lot, I was impressed with the building and grounds. It was a small church, very attractive, and had a good amount of property for growth. I walked in the sanctuary and knew immediately that this was where God wanted me to be.

I also knew that it was very difficult to find a church to pastor in Houston, Texas. I had already been advised by Union Baptist Association that for every church without a pastor there were at least twenty candidates, and that I faced a tough situation. Thankfully, the admiration was mutual, and the church voted unanimously to call me as their pastor. It was love at first sight for all of us.

Before he left, interim pastor Reverend Bailey told me of the events leading up to his calling me on the phone. "Brother Les, I received at least one resume each week. I read them but tossed most of them in the waste basket. Yours, however, impressed me because you had spent many years at just two churches, and I felt that this church needed a pastor who would stay with them."

God, in many cases, has to go around situations to get the man he wants into a church. Any pastor who has been with his congregation any length of time will tell you that God must open many doors to get the person He wants where He wants them. At this writing, I have been pastor here 31 years. It is amazing, but there were miracles involved in my being called to the three pastorates I have had. It is also amazing that all three churches I have been called to had just gone through splits and divisions, and in each case, there was a healing ministry needed. Can you begin to see why a person who abhorred arguments and detested the sort of things that cause divisions in churches was needed as their pastor? They needed someone to love and guide them.

Roslyn Baptist's congregation was very small. They could not afford to pay me a full-time salary, and since I was a bi-vocational pastor, we fit together just right. My home in Jacinto City was just

25 miles from the church. I drove back and forth at least three times a week. I was so used to driving long distances to get to the church field that 25 miles seemed short in comparison. I was very impressed with the maturity and stability of the older members, some of whom were charter members of the church, and one lady in particular. Her name was Granny Smith. She was 92 years old and never sat down for long. She loved to quote old time essays, could recite most of them from memory, and enjoyed playing hymns on her harmonica.

All three church deacons were good men with wonderful wives. Hugh Cob served as church treasurer. Hugh was an excellent bookkeeper, and I never had to worry about his job. His wife was an excellent cook. Her homemade soup was to die for. Bill Galmor taught the adult Bible class, and his wife Winnie was our W.M.U. Director. Roy Skorpenski had just retired. His wife Bobbie, with her dry sense of humor, made me laugh when she revealed that now that he was home all day, Roy wanted three square meals and was constantly underfoot. Bobbie was our Church Clerk and was meticulous about her work. She still keeps better records of membership than anyone else I know.

The congregation began to grow slowly. We were without a church pianist, and I began praying very hard for God to send us one. Unless you are very proficient, singing a cappella is very hard. We did it for quite a while. I had to lead the singing because we did not have anyone else. God's answer was to send me a teen aged girl named Pam Martin. Pam was a local girl in my neighborhood. She was raised by devout Christian parents who were members at First Baptist of Jacinto City. Her parents had her in Sunday School the first Sunday after her birth, and for the next sixteen years of Sundays after that. She had a perfect attendance record. In those days, churches gave out perfect pins for one year of perfect attendance. Pam had the pin and fifteen bars, one for each year. Her lapel looked like a general's.

Pam was very pleased with her accomplishment. Who wouldn't be? I am sure she went on occasion not feeling well. Pam learned of the open position for a pianist.

"Brother Kessler, I am not very good, but I will be glad to ride with you and Mrs. Kessler to your church and play the best I can for your services."

The members of Rosslyn Baptist fell in love with her. I had never been around a teen aged girl with so many principles. Two of the boys she dated came to me wiping their brows.

"Brother Kessler, I just cannot live up to what she expects of me".

Pam traveled with me to church every Sunday for almost five years. She married a wonderful man, had two children, and has been in contact with me through the years, even at this present writing.

## Nothing a Little Dirt Can't Cure

My love of motorcycles remained true—I had moved all the bikes I had in California to Texas: the Yamaha 650 sport touring bike and a Yamaha 400 off road dirt bike. One Saturday, June and I went for a ride. We were on the 45 Freeway heading north, and I was looking for some side road to take so we could enjoy the ride better. I turned off at New Waverly and there was a sign that read "Sam Houston National Forest". My spirits soared. The ride to the forest was beautiful. The National Forest itself was breathtaking. Up ahead I saw a shell road and decided to explore a bit. June was on the back, and she held on tight, enjoying the ride almost as much as I was.

Suddenly, a group of riders on dirt bikes came darting across the road from the direction of the woods. Was this a legal riding area? As we looped back, I noticed a large group of campers all with dirt bikes. I stopped and began talking with a young man who introduced himself as Gary K. and his group as "The Houston Trail Riders". The Riders sponsored and hosted endurance racing events about once a month. He seemed very much in-the-know, so I asked Gary if it was legal to ride in the National Forest. Gary informed me that it was not only legal, but the best riding area in North America.

"We are laying out an Enduro course next Saturday. Why don't you come and ride with us as we lay out the trails?"

The next Saturday I brought my dirt bike and found Gary. The weather had turned colder and it was raining, not hard, but steadily.

"I guess this cancels out the ride, huh?"

Gary answered, "No way, this makes the ride better!"

All my previous experience was desert type riding. That was about to change in a big way. The experience was wonderful, and I returned to camp covered with mud and a huge smile on my face.

"THIS WAS FUN."

Gary became one of my best friends, but I was also very close to many in the Trail Rider group. One special friend was Walter P. Walt was a little younger than I, the oldest of the Trail Riders, and was amazing on a dirt bike. He had been riding in the woods for over 20 years, had helped lay out most of the trails, and knew trail locations in areas most riders didn't even know existed. Walt had one special trail that led to "Super Gulley", a place he liked to bring young, cocky, hot shoe riders. This was a real test of skill. It was the deepest, slickest, muddiest I had ever seen. There were roots everywhere.

"Les when you take on this gully," Walt warned, "don't take the most obvious line because you will run into too many muddy roots on the way up. Take the line to right."

I thoroughly enjoyed watching the young riders, who considered themselves to be fast, trying to keep up with old man Walt.

Both of these dear friends are deceased. Young Gary was killed in a tragic accident; while he was changing a tire on his vehicle, another motorist swerved off the highway and hit him—killing him instantly. His family was in the vehicle while he was changing the tire. Sherry, his wife, was pregnant at the time with their second child. The older you get the more funerals you attend. I still miss them both.

My only injury on the dirt bikes came while riding with a group of friends through Sam Houston National Forrest. A vine came out of nowhere, caught me under the helmet, yanked me completely off the motorcycle, and slammed me sideways into a tree. The only place I was not protected was my rib cage and, of course, that is what hit first. I rode the rest of the day, but when I got home I knew I must have cracked a rib because every time I coughed it hurt. I went to the emergency room and had x rays taken. A female nurse came in to the examining room reading the chart. She looked up and there I sat; a bald headed old man on the examining table.

"Injured on a dirt bike!?"

I guess I gave her a big laugh that day.

My good friend John Baldwin had a heart attack at work and passed away. Our families were very close. One of John's prized possessions was a 1985 Honda Gold Wing motorcycle. The entire family wanted me to have that bike, and I was very honored to have it. I can't remember how I got it to Texas. I think John's son John

Michael rode it to Houston from California, and I flew him home. I never got to tour with the bike like I wanted to, but I did make one ride with June.

The Gold Wing was fancy; it had everything, even cruise control. But I did not like the weight of the motorcycle; it was much heavier than my Yamaha 650. Regardless, we departed Houston and rode to Argyle, a small town in Southeast Texas. Old friends, Herb and Jo Nell Perley lived there and invited us to come see their new house that Herb had built himself. Herb was one of the deacons when I was Pastor at Calvary Baptist Church in California. Jo Nell was the church pianist. The visit and the ride there and back were nice. June was a little tired, but was glad we went.

Along about this time Houston began making changes in the freeways. They began taking out the emergency lanes and installing large cement walls encasing the High Occupancy Lanes. I felt it was entirely too dangerous to ride on the freeways, and there were just too many drivers on the streets. After several close calls, I decided to sell all the street bikes and keep the dirt bikes. I had sold the Yamaha 400 dirt bike and bought a Kawasaki KDX 200, which was a wonderful bike for the woods. I also purchased a KTM 250 dirt bike which I absolutely loved.

## Stepping In

My father called me.

"Son, my mind is beginning to fail me. I can't remember a lot of things, and I am worried."

Dad was approximately sixty years old. My stepmother Thelma had passed away and he was living alone in his home in the Pineview addition of Houston.

A few years later he married a lady named Lily, but she did not live very long and passed away with cancer.

He continued, "Son, we need to go to the bank and get your name on my account because my memory is getting very bad."

We went to the bank, and on the way I asked him about the bonds he had bought during the war.

"What are bonds?"

I tried to tell him but he did not understand.

"Well dad, if you don't remember anything about them, you must have sold them some time."

"I guess that's true," he replied.

We got to the bank and added my name to his account. I found out that he had a safety deposit box at the bank. We took his key, opened his safety deposit box, and there were all his bonds he had bought during the war. They had all matured years ago and he had just forgotten about them.

"Look, Dad, here are all your bonds."

Again, he said, "What are bonds?"

"They are money, Dad."

"That's not money."

I took a fifty dollar bond and led him to the window of the bank. Dad put his name on the back of the bond, and the teller gave him the value in cash. Dad smiled.

"Now that's money. Let's do it again!"

We went back and got two more and went through the process again. I had to stop him or he would have spent the entire day cashing bonds.

In many ways dad was normal, but it was obvious he was deteriorating mentally. It was time for him to move in with his sister Adeline. She was a widow, and I knew they would get along well together. Dad moved and we sold his house. Adeline and Dad played dominos, ate well and enjoyed each other's company. Unfortunately, my father's mind continued to deteriorate and his hearing was completely gone. As a result, Aunt Adeline's grandson and wife moved in with them. Even after Aunt Adeline passed away they continued to take care of my dad. I gave them all of his Social Security and his small retirement fund for their services.

> The Masonic home is a wonderful place, and because of future developments, I wish he had gone there. They will take you when you retire, and if you become sick, they will take care of you; however, should you wait until you become ill, they won't take you. We made a mistake as future problems will show.

We went to visit my mother in the nursing home most every day. Mother's health began to deteriorate rapidly, and she passed away in October of 1982. It saddened me to watch my parents age and to try and survive in a society that had passed them by. They both thought they had planned well for this time and had enough retirement income to be able to provide for their own needs. Boy, were they mistaken. Inflation marginalized their modest incomes and made living unbearable. It just did not seem fair.

About a year later, Dad needed to go to the hospital. He was eating well, but was continuing to lose weight. I checked him in to the hospital for evaluation. The very next day I was notified that my father had expired. I should have ordered an autopsy, but did not. I truly believe that the doctors practically scared my dad—a completely deaf, confused elderly man—to death with their white coats and all the sophisticated instruments he had never seen before.

Dad passed away Dec. 31, 1983. Brother Joe Ash, his pastor, did his funeral.

# Tidbits

I found out that I was a little bit claustrophobic when I rode with Glenda in her Z-28 Camera, two-door sports car. I was sitting in the back and as I looked around I began to be very uncomfortable.

"If something happened, I could not get out of this car!"

Glenda married Stephen Seigle, her high school boyfriend, and I was asked to do the wedding ceremony, of course. They were a handsome couple, if I should say so myself, and the wedding was beautiful. Kevin Scott Seigle, my first great grandchild, was born in 1982. Everything was going great for this little family. Steve's parents, Archie and Dorothy were so pleased to have a new baby in the family.

A word to the wise; do not ever expect much attention to yourself when babies are around. Babies steal the show. It is amazing how adorable small children are. If I was called on to produce TV commercials, I would use only children and animals for all my commercials. It would sure beat the junk we see.

# 1983-1993

## Life Turns Upside Down

It was approximately 1984 when the doctors at Kelsey Seybold Clinic concluded that, since there was no other explanation for her symptoms, June was in the early stages of Alzheimer's disease.

> Mental problems seemed to run in June's family, especially in their later years. It affected everyone we knew except one aunt, Artie Fenner. June's mother—I called her 'Lady' and she called me 'Son'—suffered through a mental breakdown, and then later had a stroke that left her an invalid for about eight years. My father-in-law Bill was an attentive and gentle caregiver, but eventually he needed help. He hired a black lady named Pearlie Rooks, and she stayed with them until Lady passed away.

I accepted the analysis and followed the recommendation that June see a Geriatric Psychologist. At her first appointment, the doctor apparently asked her personal questions that she had no intention of answering. As she stormed out of the office, she informed me that under no circumstance was she ever going back. I was not allowed in the room when all this was going on, so I really don't know what she was asked, but it didn't matter—June's anger and adamancy was reason enough for me not to force the issue. I decided to wait and see how things went.

Most days, it was difficult to leave her at home alone, and on several occasions I took her to work with me. I kept my boss informed of all that was going on and he was gracious to say the least.

"Les, we need you. Just do the best you can; let us know how we can help, and take all the time off you need."

I, however, knew that my life could not continue like this indefinitely.

One day June called me at work.

"Kessler, my arm hurts."

I rushed home and found that she had taken too many sedatives and had fallen off the living room couch. Her arm was fractured and she needed immediate medical attention. Earlier, June had gone to see a physician that her mother had used and had persuaded him to prescribe her anti-anxiety medication to help her cope with irritability and over-excitement. As soon as I could, I went to visit the prescribing doctor and advised him that my wife was addicted to the medication and that he was stop authorizing refills.

One day, June and I were sitting in the front room and I noticed a strange expression on her face. She had a blank look as though she did not know what was going on. Suddenly, she fell to the floor and started convulsing. Terrified, I called 911 and the local fire department sent paramedics to our house. Before they arrived, June recovered her composure and had no recollection of what had just happened. I tried to explain it to her, but she was insistent that nothing was wrong with her. The paramedics checked her out anyway.

"Mr. Kessler, it is apparent that something is wrong and you need to get your wife to the emergency room."

June responded, "There is nothing wrong with me. Leave me alone!"

The paramedic addressed June directly, "Mrs. Kessler, we cannot make you go, but we strongly advise that you do."

She refused. They no sooner left than she fell to the floor again, and this fit was more violent than the first one. I called 911 a second time and the same crew returned. But, like the first time, the episode was over before they got there and she vehemently refused to go to the hospital. At some point, I had called June's Aunt Artie and she was now there trying to help me. A third seizure hit and again she would not budge. I decided my only recourse was to force her into the car and to take her to the hospital myself. June suffered a fourth seizure as Artie and I lifted her into the back seat. As I turned on the emergency lights and looked over my shoulder to back out of the driveway, I saw that Artie was holding June firmly, but tenderly, in her arms.

"Kessler, get us there as fast as you can."

I tried to reassure her. "I'm going to drive as fast as possible without being reckless; I'm not nervous."

I was amazed at how many motorists would not get out of the way even though I had my hazards on. At the intersection of Market Street and the I-10 Freeway, I approached a red light with a car in front of me. All the guy had to do was move up a little bit so I could merge. I honked, but he would not pull over, so I jumped the car over the curb to get on the freeway. The hospital was only five miles away, but it seemed it was taking an eternity to get there.

At one point, I vaguely heard Artie say, "Kessler, I think we have lost her."

All I could do was pray and drive. Once we finally reached the emergency room, June was immediately rushed in for examination. She was still alive. I called Ron who assured me that he would be on the next plane out of California. I called the rest of the family, and they came as quickly as they could. Our family provided so much comfort; I don't know what I would have done that day if Artie had not been with me.

June remained in the hospital for several days, and one of the many doctors attending to her was a seizure specialist from Baytown, Texas, Doctor Athari. Doctor Athari was to be June's physician and friend for many years. He was a godsend; as far as I'm concerned, he saved her life. His tests revealed that June did not have Alzheimer's disease, but that the seizures had caused irreparable damage to the part of her brain that controlled her motor skills and her ability to function socially. She could no longer clean her house, cook, or perform any of the functions she was accustomed to doing. I gave my employer two weeks' notice, and because I was 63 years old, I qualified for early Social Security.

June was prescribed *Dilantin*, an anti-seizure medication. The drug affected her in a way I cannot fully describe. She became violent, completely uncontrollable. I had to physically restrain her many times to keep her from hurting herself or me. Dr. Athari changed her medication, and she settled down somewhat.

After Ron returned home, I began to settle into life as it faced me. I thought my wife was going to die any day, but she was a real trouper and we kept "hanging in there". Although our family and friends did everything they could—brought meals, ran errands, and cleaned the house—they could not be with us all the time. I had my hands full. I offered to resign my pastorate and to help the elders find my replacement, but my church family would not hear of it and insisted that we work out this new set of circumstances together. Prayer and faith were instrumental in getting me through this difficult time.

It didn't take long for me to realize that I needed full-time assistance with June. I knew I could never put her in a nursing facility, so I prayed for a special person to help me. Almost right away, Pearlie Rooks came to mind. Somehow, I found her phone number and called her. It turns out that she was living with one of her daughters and needed a job very badly. I gave her the details of

June's condition and offered her a position that would require her to move into our home. Pearlie was delighted (as was I) and accepted the offer. I asked when she could start.

"Can you pick me up today?"

"We're on our way now!"

We picked Pearlie up that very same day. What a blessing that precious woman was to both of us, and June depended equally upon Pearlie and me.

---

Each week I put Pam Martin, Pearlie Rooks and June in the car and we drove the 25 miles to church. Our church family loved Pearlie. She was so much fun for them. Pearlie sat with June for all the worship services. She even joined our church, but Pam did not. She wanted to leave her membership where her parents attended, and I certainly understood that.

---

## Friends of Old

My friend Jim Loomis contacted me. His business was soaring and he wanted me to make more tools for him. I flew out to see him and to check out his facilities. He had moved into a nice building and was busy training employees. The future was bright for Jim, and it was good to see him so happy because he had gone through so much.

---

Jim and I had a very special relationship. He told me what he needed, I shipped it to him, and he paid my invoice. He treated me like an employee, although I was actually contract labor. Every time he gave his workers a bonus, he generously gave me one also. Our arrangement is still working to the present day.

---

In 1992, Jim Loomis rang me up with more good news.

"Les, I am in love with a wonderful woman and I would like to marry her and spend the rest of my life with her. Would you be willing to come to California and perform the wedding ceremony for us? And we want you to bring June."

"I would love to, but you understand that June has some medical problems. I will check with her doctor and see if he thinks she will be able to make the trip."

At this stage of her life, June was able to function fairly well and the doctor encouraged me that the trip might do her some good. I accepted Jim's invitation for both of us and he insisted on covering our travel expenses and making reservations for June and me at a beautiful Bed and Breakfast. As soon as we arrived, we were introduced to Jan, the bride to be—they were just a perfect match. June and I spent a wonderful week at the Bed and Breakfast with plenty of time to fellowship and to prepare for the wedding. The ceremony was held in a beautiful garden area and as I stood before the bride and groom, joined by Jim's two adult sons and Jan's adult son, I could not help but be proud of them all. By far the most impressive moment happened when the three sons all stated that they were genuinely happy for their parents. I think it was one of the best weddings I ever performed. Before leaving on their honeymoon, Jim handed me an envelope containing a check for one thousand dollars. I was astonished.

"Jim, this is too much and not necessary."

"Les, my business is going well and I insist that you take it. You and June enjoy yourselves."

While I was visiting my son in Long Beach some time later, I had the pleasure of attending a pastors' breakfast with all my former fellow pastors in that area. Now, don't get me wrong, pastors are wonderful men, but they have a tendency to stretch statistics a little regarding attendance figures and most every other mathematical equation that reflects their spiritual success—all in good fun, of course! This morning was no different and they were on the subject of weddings; the numbers performed and payments received. The usual teasing was going on, but I did not say a word. The conversation went on for a good half hour and after they had all taken a turn they looked at me.

"Les, what is the most you ever received for a wedding?"

I sat there for a few quiet seconds, bathed in false—humility.

"Oh, I don't really know the total figures, but my friend Jim flew June and me round trip to Oakland where I picked up a rental car reserved for us, drove to St. Helena where we stayed for a week at a Bed and Breakfast, and accepted a one thousand dollar check for my troubles. I think that about covers it."

Laughter filled the room, but one pastor could be heard over the noise.

"Les, I have heard some whoppers in my time but yours takes the cake."

"Believe it or not, that is what happened!"

That conversation was all in good fun, but I did feel very blessed by all of it.

---

I was still able to take June to church and the bowling alley with me. She seemed to enjoy both very much. She was totally dependent on me, and although the pressure was great, I was so very thankful that she could still go with me and we could enjoy some time together with friends.

---

## Mighty Moves

It was time for us to relocate closer to the church. I selected the community of Woodland Trails West as suiting our needs best and began making bids on several houses. None came close to being accepted. A real estate friend of mine, Richard Fallen, made a suggestion as we rode up and down various streets looking for vacant houses.

"You know, Les, sometimes you can get a really good deal on a bank foreclosure."

No sooner had the words come out of his mouth than we came upon a foreclosure on a corner lot, and he pulled into the driveway. The door had a combination lock with a telephone number on a tag. Richard called the number and was given the combination; we went inside to have a look.

The house had three bedrooms, two baths, and an attached garage. As I entered the garage I noticed that it was all sheet rocked in, including the ceiling. There were filtered vents for air conditioning and heat. It had ten neon light fixtures—excellent lighting—and even had indoor/outdoor carpeting. The garage was wired perfectly for my shop needs. I visualized where every piece of equipment would fit best.

We had paid $55,000 for our home in Jacinto City and had a firm offer of $40,000—the appraised value at the time. The house I was looking at was priced at $50,000. I made an offer of $40,000 and received a counter offer of $44,000 with $1000 at closing to use for repairs and replacements at my discretion. I closed the deal on both.

Ron came from California to help and joined all my dirt riding buddies, along with my grandson-in-law Steve. They were quite the moving crew! I don't remember who finally informed me, but they were all in agreement that my time and energy could be better spent elsewhere.

"Les, you go and do church work and we will do the moving."

I did not hesitate in my whole-hearted agreement.

My home is only three miles from the church. All I can say is, "Thank you Lord for all the moves you have made in my life and all the doors you opened for me to place me in this present situation." Friends and family are wonderful. Were it not for the physical condition of June, everything would have been perfect. It hurt to see the love of my life changing so much. It was very hard, but God provided me with someone to live in and help me, and thanks to Jim Loomis, the finances to cover it all. Praise the Lord!

The church was growing by leaps and bounds. Pam Martin, our pianist, got married, and God led Judy Dorhman to the church. Judy had a beautiful voice, was excellent on the piano, and read music very well. When she first arrived, she had not played in years and lacked confidence. Her fingers were too short, she said. God blessed her music ability and she succeeded in ways she never dreamed she would. We also called a music director, John Gundy, and started a choir. These were very fulfilling church days.

The name of the church changed to *Inwood Village Baptist Church*. I can't even remember all the reasons the deacons felt a change was needed, but obviously there were enough to make it happen.

## Recovery is Contagious

The downtown Star of Hope rescue mission—an outreach to recovering drug and alcohol addicted men—had a ranch eight miles outside of Hockley. The men at the mission who gave indication that they were serious about recovery were given an opportunity to live at the ranch and go through a three month rehabilitation program. I had obtained permission to conduct services one Thursday per month and I would take our pianist Judy and as many other church members as possible to sing, preach, and fellowship with the men. Not once did we conduct a service that we did not see at least four decisions to become Christian and several rededications to the Christian faith.

Hubert Hillman, one of the deacons at Inwood Village, had a standing bowling commitment on Thursday evenings so he was never able to participate. I really felt that he needed to go, so I asked him if he would please make plans to go one Thursday and preach the message. He reluctantly agreed. The night he finally showed up, Judy sang a special song before the sermon "I'll Talk to the Father for You". Something came over Brother Hubert. I don't remember what the sermon was about, but the man was on fire! About sixteen men came forward for prayer and confession, and the experience revolutionized dear Hubert.

"Brother Les, look what I have been missing all this time."

He never missed going again, and I let him preach every time.

## Preacher's Blessing

I taught on the Holy Spirit one Sunday, and the sermon greatly offended a church member who heard only what he wanted to hear, took what I said in the wrong way, and was very upset with me. I tried to convince him he had the wrong idea, but he then accused me of lying about it. Hubert later went to the man's house, knocked on his door, and told him how wrong he was. The man was then told that he should apologize to his pastor. Hubert set the man straight on all accounts and I was grateful for the stand he took for me.

---

So many miracles, not just coincidences, but miracles, and I want them all recorded in this book.

---

"June Kessler taught me how to pray."

A flashback: Hubert's sister-in-law had locked her keys up in her car and everyone was out in the hot parking lot trying to use coat hangers and anything else they could find to get the door unlocked. June would have none of it.

"I'm going inside to pray."

Ten minutes later, a wrecker pulled up. "Are you folks having trouble?"

Hubert asked him, "Did someone call you to come?"

"No, I was just passing by and saw all of you in the parking lot and I more-or-less knew what had happened."

He opened the door and left without another word. That was the day Hubert Hillman decided that June taught him how to pray.

"Everyone else was sweating in the parking lot getting nothing done, and June went into a cool building and prayed one prayer, and ten minutes later the car door was opened."

\*   \*   \*

Hubert Hillman was also a talented electrician who found great joy in using his skills to help others. He was like a right hand for me and his wonderful wife, Dell, was his inspiration. Dell was a beauty operator, and when it came about that I couldn't take June to just anyone because of her nervous condition, Dell began taking care her hair and nails. She and June were very close friends.

Hubert suffered from asbestos poisoning and it began to take its toll. The last time he was admitted to the hospital he asked to speak to me alone.

"Brother Les, I know I will not leave this hospital. I have prepared my family as best as I can, and I am ready to go to my eternal home."

I was touched immensely both by his dignity at death and the wonderful response of his family.

## Downhill Slide

It was so hard to watch the woman I loved slowly deteriorate mentally and physically. Having Pearlie Rooks as June's full-time companion made it possible for me to enjoy many God given pleasures: my pastoral ministry, golf, dirt bike outings with friends, and bowling in a Senior League made all the difference.

And then, Pearlie developed breast cancer and went through a mastectomy. As the cancer began to spread, it became very apparent to me that I could not take care of both women. After being with us for eight years, we moved Pearlie in with her son, his wife, and three children. Pearly shared a 10 X 9 room with a teenager and a boom box. Pearlie's health declined very rapidly at this point, and she soon passed away.

In the meantime, I was desperately praying for someone to take her place. You can't bring just anyone into your home. We had known Pearlie for years and she was like family; replacing her was going to be a major problem.

I really don't know how I managed to keep going. As many other devout Christians with even worse problems would say, "God takes you through it." My deacons helped a lot, I had good church organization, and June did the best she could.

I found two ladies in a women's shelter and tried them out with no success. They had too many problems of their own to help me with mine. All I knew to do was keep praying and carry on the best I could.

One of the ladies I bowled with, Rusty, asked me if I would go to the county jail to visit her daughter Pam. When Rusty told Pam that she had asked her preacher friend to come and visit her, Pam was not keen on the idea.

"Don't send any preachers around here. That's the last thing I want to listen to."

Undaunted, I agreed to go if Rusty would stay with June. When Pam came into the visiting room, her arms were crossed over her chest and she refused to make eye contact. More than glass partitions separated us. But she sat down, and as we began conversing with one another, her whole attitude changed. I felt so sorry for her. Her life was in a mess and she was facing possible prison time. We had a good visit and I told her I would be praying for her.

On my next visit, Pam opened up a little more. She told me she was jailed in Atlanta, Georgia, for credit card theft. Some home missionaries came into the prison and led her to Christian faith. She was then transferred to Houston county jail and was awaiting trial there. During the next several visits, I counseled with her about her life and supplied her with Christian literature which she studied diligently. I told her that she could be of great help to the other women by teaching them about Christ. We became great friends. On my last visit, she informed me that she had been given a one year sentence in a women's prison unit in another county. During that time of incarceration, we corresponded by letter.

# Angels In Dresses

It came time for Pam's release and her mother was worried because there was no place for her to go during this critical time of rehabilitation. I had been using whatever help I could get with June and nothing was working well. I spoke to Rusty about the possibility of having Pam help me for a month until she found something else. That seemed to be the answer to both of our problems. One of my deacons was a police officer, and he cautioned me about having a released felon in my home. I decided to try it for a while; after all, what could go wrong in a few days? I felt that it was worth a try. She needed money and a place to stay, and I needed help desperately.

Pam fell in love with June at first sight and was such a joyful companion for her. She helped me with the cooking and the house cleaning. Pam was with us for eight years, and all but the last year was wonderful. She decided to get married and moved away. Once again I was desperate for help.

> Pam began drinking again, and died in a terrible automobile accident while under the influence of alcohol.

Another one of my bowling teammates, Molly, had a Hispanic lady helping her with her handicapped husband. After Carl's death, Molly gave me the lady's name and highly recommended her. I contacted Elizabeth Martinez and offered her a job living with us. Elizabeth spoke fairly good English and I had very little trouble communicating with her. She accepted my offer and moved in with us.

> God gave me three wonderful women during three periods of eight years each. I don't know if the number eight has anything to do with it or not, but God certainly answered my prayers. Each one of the women was different in so many ways. Pearlie was the best cook. Pam helped me learn a little bit about computers. Elizabeth was the worst cook; however, she could make some of the dishes I liked if I guided her through the process. June and I loved all three and they loved us like family.

# Disenchanted

Church membership tends to ebb and flow. One thing that really frustrates me as a pastor is that as soon as the church gets organized and is functioning well, someone in a key position either dies or moves away. At one point, the church had grown to reaching almost 100 people in Sunday School alone, and everyone seemed happy. The downturn began when two key families moved to another city, and our youth minister began to have family problems. His wife divorced him, and soon after, they both left the church. Our pianist Judy was the next to move, and for several years there was a steady decline in overall membership. Church attendance was so low that sometimes we only had twelve people show up. June's health continued to deteriorate, and the whole of it all led me to consider just giving up. I was in a state of depression. I had never felt so negative in my entire ministry. Hugh Cobb, church treasurer, leading deacon, and personal friend came to my rescue. He put his arm on my shoulder at just the right moment.

"Brother Les, I know things have gone bad for you, but I have known you a long time and I have never seen you quit anything, and I believe you are about to make a bad mistake."

I have always been grateful for his timely help. He and his wonderful wife Mae have been at the church since it was built, and I have told them many times what a blessing they have been to me and to our church.

# 1993-2003

## Unconditional Love

Our little dog Bridget was a special gift from the family and was a constant companion to June. The black toy poodle slept with her every night. It was a familiar sight to see June lying on her right side with her left arm over Bridget who was snuggled as close to June's chest as she could possibly be. I loved to watch them and felt so thankful that something could be so dear to my sweet wife.

Elizabeth was also becoming very close to June. Her soft heart was obvious in the way she spoke, in the infinite patience she demonstrated, and in the gentleness of her touch when she helped June move.

> I am so thankful that God placed three wonderful women in our lives to help in our situation. Both Pearlie and Pam had said, "Oh, I just can't bear the thought of June dying, and I live in fear of being there when she does." June outlived them both, and it was she who did the grieving when they passed away.

I now carried a light wheelchair in the car so I could take June to church on Sunday's and the bowling alley at least once a week. It was a great effort, but I took her everywhere just to get her out of the house. There were many times that she would just as soon stay at home in her familiar surroundings, but I encouraged her to go with me as often as possible. All our family would take turns taking Mam-Maw on outings, as well—I don't know what I would have done without their love and support.

# Rest

I took June to California for a visit. While in the shower my knee gave way and I could not walk on it. I got to the doctor as soon as possible.

"Les, I have good news and bad news. The bad news is that your knee joint is so far gone that nothing can be done for it. The good news is that we can put in a new joint made out of titanium."

He showed me a group of pictures. I was happy that something could be done; however, I dreaded the recovery time and what it would do to my ability to care for June and to my schedule at church and at Trinity Company.

The operation was done at Rosewood Hospital. I was advised that I would be in the hospital for ten days which would include in-house therapy. I could then expect two more weeks of outpatient therapy.

> The patients who suffered the most pain during therapy gained the most mobility. I adopted a statement that the therapists repeated around the hospital—"No pain, no gain." When one of my therapy sessions was completed and the nurse said, "Do you want to stop here are go a little further?" I replied, "Go farther, of course, because 'No pain, no gain!'"

During my time in the hospital I often got restless at night. I would get out of bed, take my walker, and go up and down the hospital corridors visiting other patients. Many of the people I popped in on seemed glad to have company. In fact, some I was able to assure of the love of God and a few asked for advice concerning various life problems and situations. In a strange way, I actually enjoyed my stay in the hospital because it afforded me a great deal of needed rest. I was able to completely relax knowing that June was also in good hands.

# A World in Flux

It is difficult to convey how I felt as a pastor during this time of such rapid religious, political, and technological change. 'Terrorism' was becoming a household word. The widely accepted terrorist leader, Osama Bin Laden, openly declared war on the Western World. I kept hearing the term Jihad used by Islamic terrorists. Jihad was a declaration of total commitment to the destruction of the Western culture, and establishment of Islamic law. Their method was to kill enough people to get their way. It did not matter whether it was innocent people or not. America received a shock when a truck loaded with explosives parked in the basement of the World Trade Center. The driver then blew himself up—truck, building, and all. The goal was to demolish this symbol of western culture. Damage was done to the American psyche, but we recovered quickly. Every so often we would hear of a "suicide bomber" strapped with explosives, making their way into a highly populated area, detonating the explosives and themselves, and killing as many people as possible. This was a new kind of enemy to me. These people operated with total dedication to their cause, posed as ordinary civilians during the day, and terrorized the country by night.

Our president, George H. Bush inherited a real problem with Iraq. Their leader, Saddam Hussein, led his nation to attack Kuwait, one of our allies, and a war called "Operation Desert Storm" ensued. Kuwait was retaken and a temporary halt to military activities resulted.

Bill Clinton succeeded George H. Bush as president. He seemed to be doing alright until a sex scandal caused the nation to be divided again. Some thought it was nothing unusual—that other presidents had done the same thing. Others believed that his attempt to cover his sexual relations with "that woman" by lying under oath should result in his impeachment and forced resignation. His wife Hillary stood by him through it all. It seemed that we just couldn't get along about much of anything anymore.

---

June lived in constant fear that I would die before she did.

"Kessler, please don't die before I do because I don't think I could live without you."

I gave her all the assurance I could give, but she always felt afraid. Although the excitement and passion of our youth was wonderful, living life together through the good times and the bad is the real fruit of a marriage. So many of the present generation are deciding against marriage altogether claiming that the institution is no longer relevant, but I strongly disagree. I still quote the Bible in the marriage ceremonies I perform that, "what God has joined together, let not man put asunder."

---

## Joining Forces

Each Sunday as I traveled to church I noticed a mission in the strip center at the entrance to my subdivision and it intrigued me.

"Now, here we have a young congregation made up of families with children and youth renting a store front and, by all appearances, struggling to stay open—and then there's my church, debt free and only serving a few people. We ought to combine our congregations!"

I started praying about it and one day I felt compelled to stop and ask to see the pastor. I introduced myself to a man named Phil Hassel and explained my idea. He was shocked, but was glad I had come by. He agreed to join me in prayer. I discussed the possibility with my congregation and they were all excited about it.

Months passed and we never heard anything from the Rolling Creek Mission. We did receive a letter from Phil advising us that he had consulted with the Union Baptist Association and their sponsoring church. He was told that, in their opinion, joining the two churches would mean having two pastors and experience showed that this arrangement rarely worked to anyone's benefit. I decided to forget about it as a lost cause, although I had felt certain that it had been God who had impressed me to approach their congregation in the first place.

At least a year had passed when I ran into Phil at the super market.

"Brother Kessler, would you start praying about us merging again?"

I wasn't sure what had changed, but I agreed to approach my congregation again. Our churches merged in January of 1996. It was a seamless event. We dropped the names of both churches and adopted the new name of Northwest Crossing Baptist Church. Brother Phil did the preaching and administration duties and I did the Lord's Supper, preached when asked, and started a discipleship program. I was more than willing to step down as senior pastor and serve as associate pastor for as long as he would have me. Brother Phil and I never had a problem with differences in personality or perspective; we were mutually appreciative of each other.

The Hassel family was a delight. Their oldest son Paul was one of the most dedicated and committed teenagers I had ever met and we developed a strong bond of friendship. Their daughter Jamie was a delight, although her energy and enthusiasm were known to occasionally cause problems for her parents. Leslie Hassel, Phil's wife, had a beautiful alto voice and she would eventually develop a worship team that was famous for its beautiful harmony.

I was later elected Pastor Emeritus which gave me more time to devote to June and my business. I often joked about the perks of my new position.

"Now you all have to be nice to me, cannot fire me, and must cater to my every wish!"

# A Painful Discovery

I am embarrassed to say that I was showing off a little bit on a Saturday morning dirt bike ride with Jerry, Jerry Wayne, and my great granddaughter, Lacie. I made a big jump, lost my balance in the air, and landed ingloriously on the front wheel which sent me over the handlebars and flat on my back. (For the record, I know better than to ride like that.) I was embarrassed, but as soon as I had done a quick inventory and given the family a 'thumbs up', we all gave in to a good laugh at my expense.

The next morning I noticed a little blood in my urine. I wanted to ignore it, but I decided it was wiser to have everything checked out just in case. After a complete and thorough examination that was way more involved than I thought necessary given the circumstances, I was advised that I had a large tumor inside my bladder and that if it broke through the wall death would result. Immediate surgery was necessary.

The doctor's assessment of the situation was startling. "Les, that fall did something to jar this tumor and make it bleed. The crash probably saved your life."

After considering what he said, I remembered that I had no intention of riding that day. My family had just shown up, out of the blue, with their bikes ready to go. Coincidence? Not on your life!

## Horror and Heroism

George W. Bush was elected president in 2001. The Desert Storm conflict had seemingly been resolved, but the problems in the Middle East continued. Iraqi leaders were accused of many atrocities against humanity including genocide and gas attacks on their own people. Some liked the president and thought he was a good and honest man; others hated him publicly and with a passion.

On September 11, 2001, I was watching television and a news flash came on saying that America was under attack and that the World Trade Center Twin Towers had been hit by flying aircraft. All the terror and gore played out across the screen before my very eyes. I watched in horror as a jet passenger plane made a wide turn and slammed into the first building at 450 miles an hour. I could not truly comprehend what was happening. Then another aircraft made a wide circle and slammed into the second building at 500 miles per hour. I watched the confusion on the ground as people ran down ash covered streets. Servicemen were doing their best in an impossible and hopeless situation.

I noticed strange objects falling out of the upper stories. I thought at first that it must be fixtures and then I suddenly realized these were men and women jumping from the tops of the buildings to escape the smoke and flames. Then the buildings themselves began to crumble and came crashing down. The cameras switched to view the reaction in Arab countries where radical Islam was in control, and there were people dancing in the street, burning American flags, and pumping their fists in the air. I wept as I watched. It seemed like Pearl Harbor all over again. What treachery. What brutality.

The terrorists had been preparing for this operation for a long time. The pilots received their training in the United States. Oil profits had funded all terrorist activities, so money was never a problem. Osama Bin Laden himself was wealthy. At the appointed time, with all in readiness, the well planned attack took place. The third aircraft was on its way to crash into the Pentagon building. The passengers aboard had heard on their cell phones what had happened to the Twin Towers, and they determined that since they were going to die anyway they would try to retake the plane. It is impossible to imagine the heartbreak of hearing a loved one aboard a doomed aircraft calling to tell you goodbye. That is the way it happened. The passengers attacked the terrorists and made the aircraft crash in an empty field, killing all aboard.

This atrocity brought Americans together like nothing since WWII. Church services were well attended and prayers went up all over the country and abroad. Almost 3000 people died as a result of the September 11th attacks, which is about the same number of fatalities from the Pearl Harbor attack. Airline travel would never be the same. America discovered that she was vulnerable at the point of air travel, transit systems, water supplies, and computer hacking.

In response to the chaos, I obtained a copy of the Koran and began to study it. I have come to the conclusion that there are moderate and radical Muslims. The moderates say they are peaceful and had no part in the attacks. The radicals are well organized, well funded, and well trained. Training schools are going on constantly all over the world. Our government has finally begun to take the threat seriously. We now know that their ultimate goal is to kill us. America is the most hated of nations and has been called "The Great Satan".

There was (and is) a prevailing attitude that "not all Muslims are terrorists, but all terrorists are Muslims". What people do not realize is that this problem goes much farther back. As a theologian, I believe it started with the Biblical account of Abram and Sarah in the Book of Genesis, chapters 15-21. Sarah was to bear a child, but being old and infertile; she decided to help God a little bit and gave her Egyptian maid Hagar to Abraham. Hagar bore a son named Ishmael who fathered all the Arabic peoples. That is not the way God wanted it. He had promised Sarah that she would bear a son and name him Isaac and that he would be the father of the Jewish race.

The Arab world says, "Our father was Abraham, and Ishmael as the first born should have had the entire covenant blessing."

But that was not God's plan; Sarah rushed the process. God declared that He would make a great nation out of Ishmael, but clearly stated in Genesis 7:11-12 through an Angel of the Lord that Ishmael would be a wild man, a desert man. And his hand would be against everyone. And everyone's hand would be against him; that he would live in hostility with all his brothers. I think this explains why the trouble exists today.

Osama Bin Laden was named the leading enemy of America and a price was placed for his death or capture. The emotions of Americans were strongly in favor of retaliation. Our F.B.I. uncovered the names of those involved in the plot, and they were captured and tried as war criminals. Our president was beating the drums for war. He claimed that Iraq had weapons of mass destruction and should be attacked and disarmed. The leader Saddam Hussein was to be captured and tried. To attack Iraq was not a popular decision, but our President was certain and intelligence investigations assured him the weapons were there. The war with Iraq began against much public opposition. Iraq was defeated and Saddam Hussein was captured, tried and hung, but no weapons of mass destruction were found. Some said they had been removed and hidden in another country, and others said they never existed and we made a big mistake. The real problem that would drag on for almost ten years was that the Arabic insurgents came from all over the world to fight against the United States. Body caskets began coming home in large numbers. Men returned with disfigured bodies from roadside bombings. It was a terrible situation. My own great-grandson Kevin Seigle served two tours of duty as a United States Marine. We worried about him constantly. He made it safely through and was discharged when his time was up.

George Bush was elected for a second term by a highly debated vote count. Here we were again, a divided nation constantly arguing about who is right. At this time in my life I felt more than ever the conviction to be a peacemaker, but I did not make much progress. My own family was divided on political issues and it was creating a great deal of stress for me. I tried to keep June free of these worries. She knew something was wrong, but her mind did not grasp the enormity of the problems. If I could do nothing else, I was adamant about shielding her from these things.

## Coming Apart at the Seams

I developed a chronic cough and was informed that I had a small tumor on my right vocal cord and that it should be removed immediately. The fear of losing some of my voice and thus the ability to preach or sing was overwhelming. Many people were praying for me, and thankfully, the surgery went well. Every time I preached or sang from that day forward reminded me of just how grateful I was.

Sometime later, I had a little pain and discomfort in the left area of my back. I diagnosed myself as having a kidney stone and got an appointment with Dr. Selzman who had treated my bladder cancer.

"Dr. Selzman, I think I have a kidney stone."

"Well, Mr. Kessler, I think we better check it out for sure."

It turns out there was a cancerous tumor in my urinary tract, and it had to be removed immediately along with my left kidney. I knew my chances of survival were good, but why was I battling cancer so much? I did not worry for myself, but I worried about June. I was assured that she would be taken care of and the fact that I did not have to go through chemo therapy again meant I would be able to get back to her fairly quickly.

Surgery was a success, but the recovery almost killed me. I was so cold that, although the weight of the blankets was comforting, I couldn't stop shivering. The up and down movement of the wallpaper made me nauseous. (I was hallucinating and did not realize it.) At some point, an orderly stepped on one of my hoses and I thought I was going to scream with pain. From that moment on I held that hose in my left hand protectively at all times. The nurse wanted to move everything to the right side of the bed, much to my disliking.

"Leave it on the left side."

The nurse responded, "Well, it's supposed to be on the right side."

"I don't care; I am going to hold on to this tube as long as I have it." I got my way.

---

I am lucky to be alive and I know it.

---

Ron and Elizabeth took good care of June during my recovery days, but being away made it that much more apparent how quickly she was fading. It saddened me beyond belief. We could no longer take her with us when we went out, and I was forced to move a hospital bed into our room. I needed Elizabeth 24 hours a day now. I put monitors in all the rooms so we could hear June even with light breathing. There was a direct connection between our room and Elizabeth's room, and she would always respond quickly to my call for help. We learned the art of changing sheets and diapers without removing June from the bed. A therapy service came twice a week to give June some physical exercise and Elizabeth and me a break. The only downside was that we had to remove Bridget from the room because she would try to bite the therapist when she touched her beloved June.

# 2003-2013

# Losing the Love of My Life

On the evening of November 22, 2006 the event that I had dreaded for years came to pass. At about 7:00 PM Elizabeth called me to June's room. I knew she was dying. I have been around too many terminal patients not to know. I presumed she was having a stroke. I called 911 and was advised that the ambulance was on the way. The operator stayed on the line and walked me through the next steps. I was to lay my wife on the floor on her back and push on her chest in a slow, but steady rhythm. I followed the instructions and talked to June the entire time. I was certain she could not hear me, but I kept talking—hoping to reassure her, and myself as well, if possible. I told her how much I loved her, over and over.

The emergency crew arrived and started ministering to her. They placed her on the stretcher and made ready to leave. I knew that the fastest way to get the message out was to call Glenda, my oldest granddaughter, and let her contact everyone. Elizabeth was so upset she could hardly walk, but she made her way to the car somehow, and we followed the ambulance to the hospital. As soon as the doctor checked her, he came out to the waiting room and informed me that my wife was dead. Elizabeth gasped and I felt a numbness creep over me. Tracy, Gary and Glenda all rushed to the hospital to be with us, but despite the comfort of having my dear family close, I felt completely alone in that waiting room.

During all these 25 years of her illness I struggled with the anxious thought that I might pass away before June did. I never had a doubt that, if that should happen, Ron and my grandchildren would see to her care. Somehow I knew within my heart that God would not let that happen.

My family was a great help in making all the funeral arrangements. I was just not capable of making quick and wise decisions. We decided to bury June at Woodlawn Garden of Memories Cemetery, and I asked Phil to do the funeral in our church. The sanctuary was fully packed with people from all over. There were so many that some had to stand in the foyer and listen. The funeral was beautiful and Reverend Phil captured June's life with stories both endearing and humorous. The finality of the internment at the cemetery made my heart ache. Oh, how I would miss sharing life with June. The plot had been purchased for both of us, and since she passed away first, her casket was buried on the bottom; mine will be buried on top of hers.

## Learning to Live Again

Elizabeth left to stay with her nephew. Later, when my bowling and golfing buddy Bill developed medical problems that required in-home care, Elizabeth moved in with him and his daughter.

I filled my days with busy work at the church and in my shop. I got rid of the hospital bed. I cleaned out June's closet and rearranged the room. With Glenda's help, I refurnished the house and threw out everything that reminded me of that dreadful night. The new furniture made the house look nice, but it did not provide the closure I had hoped for. In the beginning, Bridget constantly looked for June. I truly believe she grieved her loss. When she finally realized she was not coming back, June's furry companion became mine. She has slept with me ever since.

Two years passed and, for some reason or other, Glenda and I decided to go the cemetery to visit June's grave. I expected to feel sorrow, but on our way there we reminisced about the fun things we had all done together. By the time we left the cemetery, we had shared and laughed with such joy, I hardly noticed the pain of my loss. It felt good and, for the first time, I realized it was okay to go on with my life. I began bowling on Friday mornings as well as with the Wednesday league. I spent more time in my shop. I rode my dirt bike with friends on several outings. If there was a social event, I took Molly. We had been bowling together for over 20 years, and I considered her my dearest friend.

## Change Leaves Room for Gain

Brother Phil was bi-vocational; he was a pastor and a police officer on the Rice University campus. He was a hard worker and I thought he took more on himself than was necessary. I mentioned to Phil that he was possibly doing too many of the day-to-day church activities and that our members were very capable people and would be willing to help if asked. He thanked me for the suggestion, but never recruited volunteers, so I guessed he had surplus time at Rice and was able to do the busy-work there.

Shortly after, I began to take notice that several groups had come to our campus for a visit within an unusually short period of time. I have been around a long time and these folks looked like "Pulpit Committees" to me. I asked Brother Phil about it and he admitted that he had been contacted by the groups, but said little else about the matter. The rest of the church seemed to suspect he was trying to leave. I couldn't imagine how that could be the case; he had such a good thing at Northwest Crossing Baptist Church.

Brother Phil announced his resignation about a month later. He confided in me that he was tired of his job at Rice University and wanted a full time pastorate. He was called to pastor First Baptist Church of Independence, Texas, on November 1, 2010 and that meant

I was once again, a full-time pastor with much to do. My first order of business was to recruit volunteers, train them, and then turn them loose to do their jobs. They were all highly talented, positive people that really enjoyed their service to the church. I vowed to serve as pastor as long as I had the health to do so, and provided them an exit strategy in the event I could not carry on.

Before Brother Phil left, we had been approached by a Hispanic group of about thirty Christians who did not own a building and were interested in renting space from us. We had agreed to allow Pastor Johnny Zuniga and his congregation to meet in our building on Sundays. They would conduct their worship service in the sanctuary while we were having Bible study (Sunday School) and then we would switch. Once I became executive pastor, we decided to offer them the opportunity of joining our church as members, and they accepted. We had all come to know and love each other, so we simply merged. Brother Johnny smiled through tears of joy.

"Never again will we be asked to move because of some reason or other. We now have a church home."

The two groups met jointly as often as possible. Brother Johnny was bilingual. I was not.

> Right now, we meet together on the first Sunday of each month and alternate preaching. We also observe the Lord's Supper on the first Sunday of each month, so when I preach, Brother Johnny does the Lord's Supper, and the next month when he preaches, I do the Lord's Supper.

One Sunday, Brother Johnny jokingly announced, "Now, Bro Les will preach to you in Spanish."

I heckled back, "If I do, it will be the shortest sermon you will have ever heard. It will be "Ola," and "Adios."

Laughter rang true and loud that day.

Brother Johnny was elected Associate Pastor and we all benefitted greatly from the union.

In order to keep up with my pastoral duties, I reduced my time in the shop by about fifty percent. This was perfectly satisfactory with Jim at Loomis Industries. I had long ago set him up by training several of his employees to do the work I was doing for them. If, and when, I could no longer do my 50%, they would be in good shape.

## The Past Catches Up

In December of 2012, my doctor advised me that I was Type 2 Diabetic and suggested I attend a hospital clinic on the treatment and the proper approach to controlling the disease. My first reaction was disbelief and then almost overwhelming discouragement.

> "Pap-Paw, you are not diabetic; just stop eating all those sugar coated donuts!" My Family

Once the initial shock wore off, I attended the hospital clinic and I was overloaded with information. Most of it made a lot of sense. I learned that although diabetes could not be cured, it could be controlled. I read pages and pages and heard lecture after lecture on how the pancreas operates, and the risks of not managing the disease. I made the decision to follow the suggestions and I entered the clinic weighing right at 205 pounds.

They just about eliminated my entire diet: No fried foods, no breads made from white flour, no sugary deserts, no junk food. All my life I had been able to eat anything I wanted, and now I was keeping track of carbohydrates! I had only ever been on one diet—in the early 1970's—when June decided she needed to lose weight and insisted that I join her. It wasn't much of a diet because I cheated. She became so disgusted with me that she gave up and never asked me to diet again.

My doctor suggested I consume an average of 1850 calories per day. I stopped eating the unhealthy things on the list and started trying new, more nutritious foods. I read the labels of every product I purchased. I joined the YMCA and their "Silver Sneakers" program. The YMCA pool was heated and I fell in love with it. I even designed my own workout. After my pool exercises, I got into the Jacuzzi and then spent a few minutes in the sauna until I was totally dry. Sometimes after completing my workout I would be so relaxed that I would take a little nap in the YMCA foyer.

I could not believe the results. I was losing one pound each day and was eating three meals and three snacks in between. I discovered I could eat almost any meat that wasn't fried. Most vegetables were okay, too. I discovered that there were brands of ice cream with no sugar added, and that sugar free deserts were not only edible, but enjoyable. I never felt hungry. Before I discovered I was diabetic, I skipped breakfast, worked straight through lunch many times, ate like a hog for dinner, and then munched before bedtime.

I went from 205 to 160 pounds and leveled off. I am currently staying between 160 and 163 pounds. My energy level is up. I feel better than I have in twenty years. If it weren't for my feet, I wouldn't even know I have a problem. (At night my big toes feel numb and somewhat bothersome and going barefooted is not an option anymore—just walking on tile floor hurts.)

After only eight weeks, I had improved to the point that my doctor took me off of the diabetic pills. My blood pressure dropped and my heart doctor took me off of all blood pressure medicine. Finding out I was diabetic gave me the motivation I needed to eat well—something I should have been doing all along. I came to realize that each of us is a product of what we eat.

# In Conclusion

Today is March 16, 2013. I will be 90 years old at my next birthday. I end this book as I began it with praise to God for a full, meaningful, adventurous life. He is so good and has blessed me far beyond what I deserve.

I am having such a good time in my later years. I am still full-time pastor at Northwest Crossing Baptist Church. I am able to play golf occasionally, and I continue to bowl in two senior leagues. I still do some diamond tool manufacture in my shop. It is wonderful to work when I want and as much or as little as I choose. Being able to simply step into the garage to do it is an additional bonus. Jim at Loomis Industries anticipates that I am planning to retire at age 90. I now feel that I would like to continue because my health is good, and I enjoy the work so much. I think I'll book a flight to California soon to talk with him about that. I am sure his position on the matter remains the same.

"Les, you can work as long as you want to."

I thank God for this wonderful friend and the many years of our association.

Every evening I thank God for another day's journey toward my heavenly home. There has been heartache and joy, success and failure, lean times and times of plenty, loss and gain. By far the most challenging of all the trials in my lifetime were the 25 years in the role of caregiver to my amazing and wonderful wife June. Through good times and bad, God provided spiritual, physical, emotional, and financial strength when I needed it the most.

And he has provided a living legacy as well; a large, extended family that I never dreamed I would have.

"Lo, children are a heritage of the Lord, and the fruit of the womb is his reward. As arrows are in the hand of a mighty man; so are children of the youth. Happy is the man that hath his quiver full of them." Psalm 127:3-5

I had a single arrow to shoot and it soared when Ron was born. Five arrows, four beautiful granddaughters and an amazing grandson took its place in my quiver. More shots were fired and my quiver became even fuller with the addition of fifteen great-grandchildren. Not many men have the pleasure of welcoming even one great-great-grandchild into the world; I have five more arrows to join the previous twenty—and still counting! I am blessed beyond belief. I have experienced immense pride being the patriarch of such a wonderful, diverse family. It has been my privilege to attend several multi-generational gatherings and my pleasure to have five generations call me Pap-Paw.

---

Well, dear reader, I think it is plain to see that God's hand is on our lives from inception to conclusion. He will have his way in any event, but he gives each of us the free will to choose. The way to God is, and always will be, through Jesus Christ; the way is open to all. The Bible is his love letter and the road map for our lives. Don't miss it.

I love you all,

*Pap-Paw Kessler (Wow! What a ride.)*

---

CPSIA information can be obtained at www.ICGtesting.com
Printed in the USA
LVOW13s0729291013

359052LV00002B/4/P